GUARDIANS OF THE VISION

PARENTING
FOR THE BIRTHRIGHT OF POTENTIAL

Anita Allen
Louise LeBrun

with 9 contributing authors

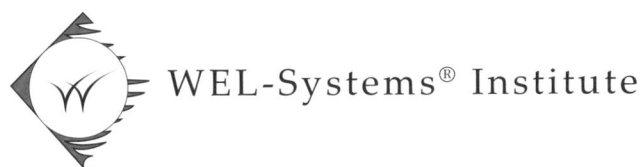 WEL-Systems® Institute

© 2009 Anita Allen, Louise LeBrun, WEL-Systems Institute

First Edition, August 2009

Published by:

WEL-Systems® Institute
260 Hearst Way, Suite 210
Ottawa, Ontario, Canada   K2L 3H1

Voice: 613-254-7218
Toll Free (Canada and USA): 1-877-233-2005
Web site: www.WEL-Systems.com
E-mail: info@WEL-Systems.com

All rights reserved.

No part of this book may be reproduced or transmitted in any form or by any means without prior written consent of the The WEL-Systems Institute, excepting brief quotes used in connection with reviews written specifically for inclusion in magazines, newspaper or the internet.

WEL-Systems®, Quantum TLC™, The CODE Model™, CODE Model Coaching™, Evolution by Intention™ are registered trademark or trademarks of Louise LeBrun, WEL-Systems Institute and are used with permission.

Library and Archives Canada Cataloguing in Publication

Allen, Anita, 1969 -

  Guardians of the vision : parenting for the birthright of potential / Anita Allen, Louise LeBrun ; with 9 contributing authors. -- 1st ed.

ISBN 978-0-9783950-4-9

  1. Child rearing. 2. Parenting. 3. Parent and child I. LeBrun, Louise, 1950- II. Title.

HQ769.A44 2009   649'.1   C2009-905241-5

To the women who are becoming new leadership models in reshaping the definition of humanity.

Also by Louise LeBrun

FULLY ALIVE:
Awakening Health, Humor, Compassion and Truth

PHOENIX RISING:
The Freeing of Human Potential

WHEN THE HORSE DIES, GET OFF...
and Stop Dragging It Around!

SEKHMET RISING:
The Restlessness of Women's Genius

For more information on Louise LeBrun and other products and experiences she is creating, please visit the web site:

www.LouiseLeBrun.com

Table of Contents

FOREWORD
 Louise LeBrun 1

INTRODUCTION
 Anita Allen 13

DANCING STARS
 Anita Allen 23

TAKING OFF THE CLOAK
 Naomi Irons-Hill 37

THERE IS NO OTHER WAY
 Amy McNaughton 49

ONE MAN'S EXPERIENCE
 Ray Landry 63

NO MORE DANCING AROUND
 Marie Smith 75

SEEING THROUGH A DIFFERENT LENS
 Lucy Hensel 85

RECLAIMING MY GODFORCE
 Pat Donihee 97

A CALL TO GO BEYOND
 Cathy Carmody 109

IT TAKES A COMMUNITY
 Debbie Elliott 123

IT'S NEVER TOO LATE
 Noreen Mejias 133

THE COURAGE TO CHOOSE DIFFERENTLY
 Louise LeBrun 147

REFLECTIONS
 all contributors 155

FOREWORD
Louise LeBrun

We stand at a critical juncture, watching our world rapidly transforming itself into that which has become unpredictable and unfamiliar yet, nonetheless, the only home we know. At this same moment, we also stand at the crossroads of great opportunity to rediscover and redefine who we are as a species, as a people and as expressions of the boundless potential that we all are. What will determine our collective fate lies in the simple act of choosing. The choices we make will determine the lives we live.

Guardians of the Vision : Parenting for the Birthright of Potential invites consideration of a new paradigm for parenting through personal experience rather than dogma. We are ready to discover and embrace parenting as a context for accelerated evolution; as a safe space within which the biological imperative of growth can easily unfold and express in ourselves and in our children. We are ready to become guardians and facilitators and invitations to greatness, allowing our intergenerational commitment to being controllers and molders and shapers to fall away. We - the parents - must become more than our histories, greater than our pasts, that we might become the seed of potential that sources tomorrow rather than that which protects history and our habits.

We must come to recognize that our greatest contribution to our children (and ourselves) is to trust our innate genius and recognize, honor and respect the potential in us all... the entelechy of being human... that lies waiting to be expressed. This approach is one that invites parents to become conduits for potential rather than harbingers of history and the status quo;

that compels parents to place themselves between children and the world, keeping at bay that which cripples and silences until the child has gained sufficient strength and voice to be able to do so for him/herself. From that place of being willing to not know; of being willing to luxuriate in the questions rather than seek quickly to select the most familiar answers that quell both agitation and curiosity; and of being willing to free ourselves from who we have been that we might become expressions of who we desire to become, potential is birthed.

I can think of no more sacred, pressing, essential and relevant expression of our humanity than what we have come to call 'parenting'. As living beings that rely on their offspring to ensure a future, this is our single, most powerful act. This day-to-day, often mindless and habituated process is the overriding force in all cultures, in all religions and at all economic levels that determines our future from one generation to the next. And yet, despite the breadth and depth of its impact, it is the process that we often engage in the most cavalier and distracted of ways. We pay more attention to the lint on our suits or the color of our car than we do to the single, most powerful and defining force that shapes culture.

Our current parenting paradigm is rarely, if ever, questioned. Grounded in the Newtonian science that dictates the norms we attribute to what a human being is and how it works, we are significantly - and increasingly, dangerously - outdated as our world becomes vastly changed by the implications of a quantum world. Our willingness to embrace the underlying paradigm of a quantum world while staunchly holding to a Newtonian parenting paradigm generates a dichotomy of the soul; a schism that leaves us 'doing' things to and with our children that we know, deep inside where we live, does not honor the truth of who and what we are. And yet, in our mindless fear and uncertainty, we continue to rush headlong to the edge of the cliff. The problem with this is that our children don't get to choose - they must follow our lead.

Foreword

Parenting is the gift that keeps on giving, from one generation to the next, shaping lives and harnessing the creative Life Force that will either feed our souls or destroy them. In this moment, the choice has become more imperative than at any other time in history as we face massive, expansive and unforeseeable change. We - the adults - are the ones who must reclaim the territory of our own inner landscapes that we might find our way back to honoring the magnificence of who we, and our children, intuitively are.

The Bigger Picture

In my 20-plus years of working with both men and women, I have witnessed a species that cannibalizes its young. Although we may not consume the flesh of their small bodies (and even that's up for grabs when we know there are those who offer their children as sexual partners in exchange for money and their own freedom), we most definitely have become adept at gobbling up their innocence, their spontaneity, their sense of play and ability to trust, leaving a mechanically functioning yet vacuous, spent and empty device to move through the requirements of living.

In my work, I have been astounded over the years by the number of high-functioning, outwardly 'successful' men and women whose bodies and lives carry the long-buried and desperately forgotten truth of a past filled with disrespect, denigration and, in many cases, brutality and terror. "Children don't remember", we like to tell ourselves. "It's not a big deal - they don't really care', is another lie we cling to in our desperation to justify the unjustifiable to ourselves.

Daily, we learn of increasing numbers of children and young adults moving through the world as living expressions of the utmost desperation (street children, AIDS orphans, dropouts, runaways, etc). These, we can easily identify. What is not so easy to identify are the ones who live in attractive homes and wear nice clothing yet their young lives are rife with the same fear and desperation.

Disease in our children - from Type 1 Diabetes to ADHD to early-onset asthma to autism - is relentless in its pursuit of those that are the life force of sustainability of the species. Behavioral challenges - from bullying to battering by and amongst children - is leaving its mark on both its victims and its perpetrators. Sexually active 9 year olds and increasing numbers of teen pregnancies surface in our awareness as do rising incidences of violence against young girls by their boyfriends. Strategies for coping with their young lives, as exhibited by children from as young as 5 into their early teens, include drugs, alcohol and suicide.

These children - our children - are screaming at us to pay attention! They are desperately trying to make their way through lives that aren't working, devoid of any sense of how to make them better and so seeking to make them disappear. A sense of hopelessness and despair has hardened into a veneer of aggression and a strategy of first-strike. Potential no longer lives here.

There is no mystery to why our children are in the shape they're in; why children, adolescents, teens and young adults are so filled with hatred (of self and other) and rage. Simply put, we have made choices. Whether those choices were made as their parents or their teachers; whether they were made as their coach, choir master, babysitter or religious leader, we have been making the choices that have imposed life on our children like a sentence to be served, forcing them to become the consequences of our actions/inactions. The evidence is mounting that we have failed them, miserably!

I can't think of a more important conversation than this one. Nor can I think of one that is more venomous or combative. The playing field of 'parenting' is riddled with land mines of history and habits, rights and righteousness, and the abject terror that comes with the notion of losing power and control. It is a conversation that few dare navigate since this practice is the very hallowed ground on which stands the notion of 'family' and all that it entails. With hand over heart and flags waving, we hide behind the 'noble cause' and the myth of the intact family to keep at bay the scrutiny that would, without doubt, show up the lies and betrayals for what they are: the sad legacy of our own treacherous journey to adulthood. In many cases, we may be tall enough to qualify for adulthood but nonetheless harbor an angry and terrified child, within. Nonetheless, we are long overdue for calling up our courage and our innate truth to guide us through these seething waters.

The Process of Parenting

Parenting, as a process, hides behind an unchallenged veil of being untouchable... a 'sacred cow' badly in need of a BBQ!... and holds sufficient power to cause us to back away, look away and seek to change the subject. So much of the dogma of parenting falls from the dogma of 'god and church' ; that to question one is to challenge the so-called inalienable rights/power of the other. To take on the process of parenting is to take on the legitimacy of any external reference, including the one that comes from on-high. For many, that is a frightening place to stand, not just because of the inner turmoil but because of the external pressure and leverage exerted by the collective to remain blind, deaf and mute. How dare you think for yourself! How dare you see what you see, hear what you hear and know what you know! How dare you speak the truth of your own experience without benefit of the agreed-upon filters of the collective 'truth'! In these, we must find the strength within ourselves to stand tall and, often, to stand alone.

Do we really want to know what we've done to our children? Do we really want to know what has been happening to our children - all of our children... the ones we birthed and the ones that live elsewhere - when the truth can be so ugly? Do we really want to know how we have or that we have been a part of this outcome, whether by intention with the raising of our own hand or by abdication, as we stood by and said or did nothing? Without a willingness to know, we have no alternative to the mind-numbing, soul-sucking practices that have brought us to where we are today. Without a willingness to know, the key to transforming it all - us! - remains inaccessible. And indeed, in this, the truth shall set us all free.

What we've come to consider 'parenting' is a vastly mixed bag of great and far-from-great experiences that have accumulated in the lives of our children. Its underpinnings lie in the notions of blood lines (breeding) and ownership (*my* children, *not my* children), most frequently depicted as biological children through a birth process or children appended to an existing family (i.e. husband/wife/partners/mates) through adoption. That pretty much sets the boundaries for what typically qualifies.

The ability to breed - to physically conceive, bear and birth children - has little connection to parenting. The fact that we can procreate does not in any way indicate that we can engage to create lives worth living! Far too many who produce offspring are incapable of nurturing potential; and many unable to produce offspring are both willing and able to nurture potential. They are related and not necessarily connected.

Children in our presence through these processes are considered 'ours' and we then are considered responsible for them. We are responsible for their physical needs (shelter, food, clothing) as well as their socialization (good manners, appropriate behaviour, schooling, etc.). Following these two primary considerations sometimes comes attention to emotional and spiritual needs. However, here's where it gets more complex, given that we can't give what we haven't got.

Children are at the mercy of their environments and the people in them. At the age of 5, they cannot choose to leave home and launch a new life. It is the adults in the lives of those same children who carry the power and the resources to redefine *themselves*, that they might engage differently in the presence of the next generation. But in order for us to do that effectively, we must first come to terms with our own experiences of having been parented; and to do that, we must be willing to allow ourselves to know the truth of our own experience.

'Parenting' is the gift that keeps on giving. Its impact is intergenerational and blindly unchallenged. A nominalization, 'parenting' is a code word that we use to refer to a common experience that we share with others. We have notions of 'good' parenting and 'bad' parenting but according to what standard? The beliefs, values and attitudes to which we subscribe - typically passed down from one generation to the next, reinforced through church and community - become the framework around which the practice of 'parenting' will shape itself. When was the last time we actually stopped and paid any attention to how those beliefs/values/attitudes came to be? How long has it been since we paid attention to our relationship to these, whether having chosen them or suffered their imposition some long time ago? Just how deeply buried are the memories we carry of our own childhood and the impact of those parenting practices, on us?

Parenting, as a process, is long overdue for being explored, discussed and carefully scrutinized for the powerful impact it has on the adults all of our children become, far beyond the boundaries of blood lines and ownership. Our notions of 'parenting' are desperately in need of a new paradigm... a new context within which to consider ourselves and our offspring... that we might find a new place to stand and from which to consider potential - ours and theirs. Around the world, and in our own backyards and school yards, children are living horrific lives and becoming the adults that shape the next generation. In this simple truth, we find ourselves in deep trouble.

A WEL-Systems® Journey

For decades, books have been written on parenting; 'how to' guides that have told us what we (those in power, with control) must do to shape our children (those powerless, being controlled) lest they be left to their own devices and wreak havoc in our nicely organized world. What all of these have in common is that they focus on what the adults must do with and/or to the children to produce specified outcomes; and that the ultimate measure of a successful parent is their ability to cause their children to conform to some pre-determined framework for living.

What has long been missing from the parenting conversation - until now! - goes far beyond what behaviors our children should or should not be permitted to express. We require a recognition of the fundamental power that lies in the parenting process to shape and define culture; as well as a broader, more compelling place from which to explore and redefine parenting, itself. A WEL-Systems perspective offers a journey of discovery that makes room for both of these to be discovered and embraced, with outcomes that go far beyond incremental change!

The stories in this book represent the journeys of self-discovery in the lives of those who have written them and the natural fallout from this evolution on engaging with children. In these pages, you'll find the truth of those who, through their WEL-Systems experiences, recognized that unless they reclaimed themselves, they had little to offer their children in the unfolding of that unique and individual potential.

These courageous ones took the risk and have chosen not to hide their own truth and their own uncertainty behind the generations-old habits that pass for raising our children. They have chosen to be truthful, first with themselves and then with their children and others in their families. They have become willing to come face-to-face with themselves and become willing to risk disapproval of their communities and their peers, choosing to live their lives from an internal truth rather than an external authority. In doing so, they have awakened to the simplicity and strength of their own inner truth as the place to stand in sustaining and expanding that awakened truth in their children. Without it, we have nothing meaningful to offer. We can only repeat what is already there.

Foreword

Those sharing their lives with you in these pages have moved far beyond the notion of parenting tied to bloodlines and ownership and have come to know that the power of parenting resides in becoming the guardians of the vision of what's possible for all our children. They have come to know and reclaim respect, integrity and generosity of spirit (RIG) for self and other; and its natural consequence of nourishing the birthright of potential - for each, unique individual child as well as the species. First, nurture the Self. Then and only then is it safe for the naturally occurring potential in the child to be explored and expressed. We must find the courage to become the 'more' that we seek in order for it to take root in the world of our design.

What you'll find in these pages is hope! As you read, you'll gain a sense not only of what's possible but also how you might find it in and for yourself. *You* are the person who has more power and leverage in your child's life than anyone else. In the invitations for you to pay attention to yourself, you'll find opportunities for you to notice *you* for a change and not your children; and to get curious about who you are, how you move through your world and what your legacy will be with the small people who look to you to define their world. Perhaps the most important question you'll be encouraged to ask yourself is: would you want to be parented by you?

Children as the Seed of Potential

In each child lies the seed of their own unique, individual potential, like the entelechy of an acorn to become an oak and not a spruce. But far beyond that, collectively, our children *are* the seed of potential for the evolution of the entire species. Unless we find a way to open the parenting process to go far beyond history, bloodlines and ownership, our very existence is in great peril of accelerating in an ever-descending spiral of decay and self-annihilation. This is not something that we do only for our children - it is what we must do for ourselves.

We need to recognize that our children - all children - are the seed of potential for the species. In all ways, their evolution is the only possible guarantee of our own evolution. If we cannot find within ourselves what it takes to allow our children to become more than we are; to express new ideas and ways of being; to carve out new space for themselves in ways that allow them to be authentic and present, internally referenced and willing to create a new world; if we cannot open ourselves to learn from and be shaped by our children, then we are destined to continue to repeat the mistakes of the past, all in the name of good behaviour and civilization.

We need to begin by taking a long, hard look at ourselves; at the degree to which the things we say do or don't match the truth that our body carries. We need to come to terms with the rage and fear that our own histories offer up, allowing ourselves to own and move through what has for far too long kept us locked into the loss of our own innocence and the roiling resentment of innocence in any other. Only then, are we able to make room for our children to be expressions of that in our lives.

We need to wake up! As Gaia intensifies her message to us, so do our children intensify their messages to us. Their rage and outrage fills their bodies with tsunamis of bullying and battering each other; with eruptions of aggression directed at self (suicide) and other (murder); and with wave after shock wave of abdication from their own lives through disease, drugs and alcohol... at younger and younger ages. We are long overdue for pushing the re-set button on our continued ability to thrive as a species.

The planet itself is letting us know that we have gone too far! It is rising up and taking back its potential, paying no mind to what we think it should or should not do. It does not consider, it simply responds to what we have created. So it will be with our children.

Children by choice. Children by accident. Children by obligation. Children by surprise. Children by acts of curiosity, acts of love and acts of violence. Children are the most powerful evidence we have of our existing inability to recognize that parenting is how we have consistently carved out the future by mindlessly repeating the fast. Parenting redefined and redesigned can become the invitation to let go of our own rage and terror; to reclaim our own innocence lost or taken and let go of the vengeance evoked, that we might STOP repeating the pattern.

In the essential genius of who we are as phenomenal expressions of the Life Force, there is always hope. What we need now is to find within ourselves both the willingness and the ability to own what we have created that we might stand tall and create again. We're running out of time to make the course corrections *to ourselves* that are essential to carving out new paths for our children. The only time we have that will make a difference, is now.

INTRODUCTION
Anita Allen

There are days – today is one of them - when I wonder what on earth was I thinking when I conceived of this book project. I am no expert by the usual standard. I have no degrees, no pedigree in child psychology. I only have the 'street cred' that comes from raising three boys - and in many circles, that would be less than impressive. So far today I have broken up at least one epic skirmish over toys, attended a parent-teacher meeting about my son's sudden urge to blurt out "penis" during circle time and, at this very minute, my offspring are exuberantly thundering through my office like a herd of stampeding buffalo. Somebody call 'Nanny 911'!

But wait a minute! Even if the bespectacled nanny were to arrive cloaked in her cape and superior manners she would have nothing revolutionary to offer me. In fact, she would be bringing more of what is already available. In these days of reality TV and hip Internet sites, there is a dazzling array of information about how to parent more effectively. Even though this information looks different on the outside, drill into it and you will discover that not much has changed in the conversation about parenting for decades.

All the information that we have available to us on the topic of parenting has been created within a worldview that has some fundamental 'laws'. These are the suppositions we have about reality based on concepts that have continued unquestioned into our modern day life; in spite of mounting scientific evidence that continually illustrates that this worldview is incomplete and far too narrow to accommodate our human experience.

We have always seemed to favor the familiar even when it ceases to serve us. Change - particularly sweeping fundamental change - terrifies us. We have a choice to free ourselves from outdated worldviews and restrictive dogma but many of us don't know it.

Generation after generation has vowed to improve on our methods of parenting. The best we have been able to do is to choose based on our own experiences of being parented what we will continue to do - or not do - to our own children. All this, only to have that dreaded moment that nearly all of us will experience when you open your mouth to hear the one thing you vowed never to say to *your* kids - pop out! It has happened: you have become your mother/father. It turns out that will power and determination to be different are not enough. In the parenting conversation all that has been available is the same information rearranged and reformatted, generation after generation. Folks, we are rearranging the deck chairs and the Titanic is sinking!

Our world is changing with an intensity and acceleration that is hard to ignore. We are living in an age where climate change isn't just a theory in science class, it is happening. The polar ice caps are disappearing, the sea levels are rising and there is mounting evidence that in our children's life time, and perhaps even during our own, our planet may undergo a pole shift that will quite literally turn our world upside down.

Everywhere we look there is a crumbling of what we have known. Change is coming fast and furious, on a global scale; affecting everything from our health, as pandemics easily circle the globe, to our finances as economies teeter worldwide. This is the world we are giving our children - and we are providing them with outdated information as the means to navigate it.

What is this information, you might wonder - and I don't blame you, as it's so embedded in our self-concept and our structure of reality that it is akin to asking a fish "How's the water?"

Introduction

When it comes to the conversation about parenting, our current belief system is built around the following:

- There are qualified experts 'out there' on everything, including your children. They are right – you are wrong.
- As a parent in your child's life, YOU are the expert, not them. That makes you right and your children wrong.
- There is a range of 'normal' that is desirable, whether it is developmental milestones or behavior. If you or your children fall outside of that range, there is something wrong that needs to be corrected.

Overt discipline of children is no longer 'fashionable' in the form of physical discipline however, that has done little to change our methods of command-and-control parenting. These days, discipline shows up along the spectrum of verbal battering, humiliation, threats of abandonment/exclusion, coercion, bribery and manipulation - with the intention of ensuring our children meet some culturally referenced range of 'normal'. We want to mold them into the models of behavior that we have established so that they fit in and don't rock the boat. We homogenize them.

I don't know about you, but being homogenized and learning to be a mascot for the status quo has not served me well in my life. Oh sure, I was a successful and competent adult at first glance; and beneath that carefully crafted and highly rewarded façade, I was dying a slow death. I had learned to distrust myself and not only defer to external expertise about every aspect of my life but to actively seek it out. I was cut off from my unique identity and when I wasn't performing like a trained seal (a highly functioning one, I might add) then I had no clue about who I really was. I do not want my children to live the same fate. If I can spare them the 30-odd years it took me to re-discover and reclaim my own unique potential and connection to who I really am, I am willing to do so, no matter what it takes.

As it turns out, all it takes is an open mind and a willingness to trust the innate wisdom that resides in each of us; and then to make choices about our lives that are guided by that wisdom. No effort or struggle required! Enter Louise LeBrun and her ground breaking, courageous creation, The WEL-Systems® body of knowledge. This is a source of new information. This body of work introduces something we didn't have access to before. It's like offering the captain of the Titanic a GPS and high level sonar system to detect the iceberg. No need to rearrange deck chairs in this scenario! And as in this metaphor, it simply requires a willingness to explore new science and new perspectives about what we have held to be our reality. As it turns out, there are lots of different 'realities' and 'truths' – rather than one that is singular, absolute and all encompassing.

The WEL-Systems body of knowledge combines the latest information available from the fields of quantum science and biology; along with an understanding of the deep structure of language and the predictable patterns of thought, from the field of Neurolinguistic Programming (NLP); to offer a sum that is *much* greater than its parts. Elegant in its simplicity, it offers a context for profound change.

In a WEL-Systems context, we discover that we are organic by nature. This seems obvious and yet for centuries we have been treating our bodies as though they were machines rather than embracing the fact that we are actually organic processors. What we process is the energy and information that accompanies our experiences. All emotions and thoughts carry neuro-chemical and electric energy as impulses move through our brain/body, forming thoughts and reactions/actions. If we shut off the process, this energy remains leftover to be processed at another time. We have been taught, in a variety of ways, to shut down this process mid-stream and to brace against it. For example, when was the last time you honored the urge to cry at

Introduction

the office, the grocery store or during a parent-teacher meeting? The longer we keep this stuff locked down, the more likely it is to show up when we least expect it; and when we feel that it is 'inappropriate' based on the rules of what is deemed acceptable public behavior.

My son's explosive outburst during carpet time at school was a perfect example of this. In the last two years, he has gained two little brothers; has had four different teachers due to staffing changes at his school; and our recent move to a new community has landed him in a new class with yet another new teacher. The pressure of all this enormous change was boiling over in his body. He blurted out the one word he could find that would swiftly get him ejected from the confines of the classroom out into the hall, where he could get some breathing space.

In an old paradigm, I would not only been horrified but punishment would likely have been swift and decisive. I'd have been cringing with shame during the parent-teacher conference and I would never have dared to show my face at PTA meetings, half expecting to be ostracized and whispered about as the mother of "the penis-yelling kid". From where I stand now, I was able to use this as an opportunity to first, teach my son how to breathe deeply and relax into the energy and information that was building to a crescendo in his body, defying language. Once his body stabilized, then I was able to have a conversation with him about his experience of change and together we found alternative ways for him to get what he needed to feel comfortable. These alternatives were discussed with his wonderfully supportive teacher, who has been willing to 'think outside the box', and they were implemented. My son now has the opportunity to honor the energy and information moving in his body, taking a moment to process it as he needs to. It is quick, simple and effective – and he doesn't need to shut down any part of himself.

More than discovering that our bodies are organic processors, designed to process energy and information from our experiences, we are spiritual beings inhabiting physical bodies. If this is a new concept for you, I encourage you to stay with me for a few more seconds, take a deep breath and allow yourself to consider, perhaps even be reminded, of who you are beyond the trappings of roles and responsibilities that we wear like they are our 'real' identities. The essence of each of us is spirit and this perception of our true nature has become evident in science (check out the research of Dr. Bruce Lipton for more information). Call it what you will – Higher Self, Authentic Self, spirit, god force, signal - intuitively, we know this about ourselves. Over time and under the pressure to conform to the expectations of others we forget and then many of us wonder why we aren't fulfilled in our lives. Our essence is the intangible quality that makes each of us uniquely individual.

Children have this in spades. I have seen people nearly drive off the road trying to get a glimpse into the stroller to see my kids. Why? Because babies fascinate us. Their newness shines out of every pore. Their innocence and wonderment are undiluted. They embody joy and connection. They are filled with potential. They remind us of hope and possibility. Even a glimpse from a passing car will bring a smile and brighten a stranger's day. This is the power of raw potential.

This potential is present in each and every one of us – it is our birthright. Sadly, for many of us this has been gradually eroded by a culture that values conformity over the inherent individuality embodied by those who are closely connected to their essence. Even more tragic is how many of us have had that innocence and joy ripped away from us and devoured by another to slake their thirst for what they were robbed of, perpetuating a cycle of violence, denigration and exploitation.

The buck stops here. We are the Guardians of Potential. **You** are a Guardian of Potential!

Introduction

As an adult, it is not too late to reconnect to your own potential – in fact; it is a necessary step in becoming the guardian for future generations. You simply cannot give what you haven't got. You also can't be effective if you are operating from an outdated worldview or context for living. A broader perspective, a different lens, is required in order to stop needlessly restricting the power and possibility that each of us carry as our birthright. WEL-Systems offers you a brand new perspective to consider and is the source of information that is completely new in the field of human potential. New information is critical if we are to avoid endless repetition of our past.

It isn't necessary to have children to be a Guardian of the Vision. We are all a part of the sacred whole that makes up our world and we each can make a difference, individually and collectively. The brilliance of you simply being 'You' creates a ripple that spreads and ultimately touches each of us – adult and child.

In the stories that follow you will meet an amazing cross-section of people who have reclaimed their birthright of potential. Some are parents and others have not given birth to children but have given 'birth' to their own unique potential and in doing so, have made an undeniable impact on those around them.

As you have already surmised, this is a far cry from a traditional "How To" guide about parenting children. There are no strategies, no steps and no rules. This is a book that offers you new information and a new context to consider who you are as an individual and from that awareness, to consider who your children are. It invites you to embrace imperfection and to seek out the genius that it represents. It encourages you to become fully alive so that you can find a way to help children remain connected to their enlivened essence, ensuring they will not only know that they can shape their world but will have the capacity to do so - making it a reality rather than a wish or hope. I believe that our children are the future and as such, are a precious resource.

Now, back to my 'precious resources', who are tearing around the house with unbridled enthusiasm. I'm going to spend some time being reminded of how to play and I hope you will continue your journey through these pages that are filled with joy, hope, wonderment and reminders of your potential. I sincerely hope you heed the call implicit in these pages to become a Guardian of the Vision.

DANCING STARS

Anita Allen

"One must still have chaos in oneself to give birth to a dancing star"

F. Neitzsche, Thus Spoke Zarathustra

The pain came as wave stacked upon wave with no space between. I crumpled in on myself, completely terrified of what was going to happen next. Gasping, I was beyond tears. I can't recall ever having been so afraid, vulnerable or out of control. I was having a baby.

I went to all the classes. I had seen the videos. It appeared that everything that I had learned about birth was a euphemism for what was actually happening. This was NOT how it looked in the movies. Did that mean there was something wrong? Was I in danger? Was my baby?

Every pelvic exam done by an indifferent physician felt like a violation. Each part of the procedure to prepare for birth was an indignity. The nurse was ending her shift and had no patience or energy left over to offer comfort to a frightened first-time mom. I was left with the feeling that I was a 'drama queen' rather than being seen as a woman overwhelmed by fear and pain. A woman who arrived exhausted by the life I had lived prior to that moment; a woman who was emotionally and spiritually bankrupt.

The shift changed and a new nurse arrived. Taking me in at a glance, she sat down beside me and gave me the gift of her full and complete attention. She showed me how to match the rhythm of my breath with hers. She held my hands and looked into my eyes and saw ME. I knew I could trust her and she began to teach me how to trust myself.

Giving birth to my first child was a traumatic and terrifying experience. One that to this day evokes tears as the residual energy of that experience, nearly eight years ago, moves like a wave through my body. Relaxing, I soften my belly and breathe, riding the wave, trusting the insight that will be born in the next moment. It was not always this easy.

For weeks and even months after giving birth, I walked around in a daze. The unexpected intensity of the physical pain, the confusing changes in my body and the healing that was taking place left me feeling like I was living in a stranger's body. I was sleep deprived and my unrealistic goal of resuming my frenetic pace as a small business owner only days after giving birth was exhausting. It seemed that every time I relaxed and tried to sleep, I would re-live the scene and the terror I felt; a movie on the screen of my eyelids.

I felt dysfunctional and I berated myself constantly to just get over it. Plenty of women had given birth. There was nothing exceptional about my experience - I was healthy, my baby was healthy. Everything went according to plan. I didn't understand why I felt so broken. I didn't want to tell anyone what was going on; to let anyone see how I was floundering. Everything about my self-concept in those days had to do with being competent and in charge; steady and stable. I was unwilling to give up the last vestiges of who I was pre-birth and I was hanging on to those fragments of my old identity like debris from a shipwreck. Without them, I believed I would drown for sure. In the course of 24 hours, my life had become unrecognizable.

A Sinking Lifeboat

At one point in my life, I had given up hope of ever becoming a mother. After years of monthly anticipation followed by disappointment; after exploratory surgery, painful tests and a brief taste of the rigor and invasion of infertility treatments, I had decided that I was defective. Motherhood clearly wasn't for me. My friends were getting pregnant and they began to orbit around their children. It was easy for me to remove myself from their lives, quietly slipping out the back door of long friendships, keeping my sadness to myself.

I poured all of my energy into creating my Physiotherapy practice; regularly working long hours. I fussed and fretted over every aspect of it like a mother hen. I invested emotionally in my clients and my staff, allowing all of my 'mothering' energy to find an outlet through the misguided nurturing of everyone but myself. It was unhealthy and exhausting. In order to distract myself from the situation I was unconsciously creating, I decided to open a second clinic and poured even more of my effort into that. It was the only way I knew to deal with my emptiness.

By the time I discovered I was pregnant, I was in the middle of a major expansion of both clinics. Negotiations and conflicts were part of my daily routine as I hounded tradesmen to ensure they fulfilled my vision, all the while dealing with legal snafus and zoning issues. I moved ahead on pure will power, ignoring the fact that inside I was screaming, "STOP"! I was accustomed to silencing every internal cue that felt the least bit uncomfortable by working harder – and that was what I continued to do right up until the day before I delivered my son.

Looking back now, I know I wanted so badly to stop and enjoy the gift of my pregnancy but I felt there was no way out of my obligations. After years of dodging the chaos surging through my body and ignoring the conversations in my head that were running counter to the ones that I was having out loud, the moments when I was still and silent unleashed frightening thoughts and feelings - I avoided it at all costs. Being busy distracted me. It fed the illusion that I had created – an illusion I was clinging to like a lifeboat because without it I had no clue who I was.

Care & Feeding Of The Yet To Be Born

By the time I was in labor, my body was alien territory. Everything I had been running from was locked inside me, like an overstuffed closet with the contents poised to fall out if anyone dared to open the door even a crack. Also locked inside was my soon-to-be-born son. He listened and reacted to those angry exchanges with lawyers and tradesmen. The energy and information contained in every thought or emotion I experienced was shared with him as his nervous system was developing. During my pregnancy, I took all the prenatal vitamins and put the 'right' foods into my body. I gave up coffee and alcohol. I avoided chemical cleaners and processed food. What I never even considered until a WEL-Systems® program was what else I 'fed' my unborn child.

My son was nearly two years old when I began to explore new information through WEL-Systems. During a conversation in my first program, I realized how my son was a reflection of my life experience when we discussed the research of Candace Pert. I learned that all of our thoughts and emotions are communicated through our body and nervous system by hormones and neuropeptides; these are the molecules of emotion. This new information instantly resonated because I understood the science behind it and the evidence was right in front of me in my child's behavior. Before his birth, he was literally bathed in my fear, my ambition, my desperation, my anger, my need for control. The first time I gave him crayons to color with, he painstakingly lined them all up on his highchair tray without ever picking one up to explore, play or create with.

My first reaction to the realization of how my experiences had been shared with my unborn son was devastating guilt. Mercifully, the moment was brief as I sat among my peers in a WEL-Systems program and allowed myself to claim the enormous wave of energy and emotion that engulfed me. Breathing deeply and relaxing into my inner chaos, my body did exactly as I was learning to trust it to do – it simply processed the energy in much the same way it would deal with hiccups. When it was over, I no longer felt the need to blame or beat myself up for being a failure as a parent; for not being a good mother. I had insight about how to move forward armed with this new information. I understood with much more clarity what had been a driving force in my relationship with my young son, and it had everything to do with me.

This discovery has been a cornerstone to my ongoing journey as a parent. When I recognize myself in my children's behavior, I see it as an invitation to deal with my own issue, first; and then I openly model my discovery. I show and explain to my children how to relax their bodies, how to trust themselves and embrace their imperfection. Parenting in this way challenges me to become more, creating the space for my children to continue to expand into. Our lives are far from picture perfect by someone else's standards – AND they are endlessly interesting.

Rage, Resentment & the Myth of Motherhood

One of the gifts of my oldest son's life experience so far is his incredible intensity. He is very funny and creative as well as being committed and focused on what he is passionate about. However, it also means he lives in a state of high drama and has an acute sense of injustice. That same focus that works so well in some areas of his life can drive me to the edge of madness – almost. This is when remembering to breathe deeply becomes a useful tool, indeed.

Much of the irritation that gets evoked in me has to do with my own feelings of discomfort. When I take a moment to take a deep breath; to relax and to ponder what underlies that simmering caldron of irritability, I see what personal need I have pushed aside in order to accommodate someone else. Sometimes it's as simple as needing to go to the bathroom – which, by the way, is a great place to find a moment to be alone! Other times I notice that there is something else needling away at me under the surface that I have been ignoring. In those instances, my son is simply becoming a target for what

I am not dealing with. There have also been moments when I am overwhelmed and exhausted, and his freedom ignites a longing for the same in me; and my irritation threatens to boil over into full-blown rage. None of this has anything to do with him – it has to do with me.

Rage and motherhood aren't two words that we comfortably think of together however, I believe it's an aspect of parenting, much like the birth process, that we gloss over. In fact, we often deny its existence vehemently. I have experienced the effects of the energy of rage ignored in my own life and in the lives of the clients that I work with as a CODE Model Coach™ - and it is very real.

We have so many negative associations with the word rage that some of us physically flinch when we see it in black and white. Rage is a code word for an intense body experience. Rage doesn't exist as a 'thing' – it is a description of an internal state that has lots of what I will call 'fire' energy as its signature. Fire energy is much easier to talk about without judgment. Fire energy is intense. It is the energy of creation, of passion; as well as being the energy of destruction, anger, irritation – and rage.

As an internal state, the fire energy that accompanies rage can be processed within us without venting it on anyone. This is not the same as locking it down, pasting a smile on your face and eating another cookie, having another drink or taking another pill to try to keep it from spilling out.

We are capable of doing incredible harm to ourselves or to others when we ignore the energy that is seeking resolution in our own bodies. Claiming the energy of rage is easy. It is as easy as learning to trust your body to process it. It is as easy as choosing to take a deep breath, letting yourself relax those clenched fists, that tight belly, those shoulders that are bunching up, knowing that your body can efficiently deal with what is in flow inside you. You might feel hot, prickly, and/or itchy. You might notice your breathing pattern change or that there is a flurry of sensation in your body. You might even cry. And in a few short moments, your body will stabilize, the internal activity will be over and there you will be, with a sense of calm and the capacity to move forward differently. Fire energy is not something we need to fear in ourselves or to judge or be judged about.

As a mother of young children, I know the toll of sleepless nights; of endless demands on your time, attention and energy. I know what it is like to feel like your entire identity has fallen to bits in a mere 24 hours, leaving you to pick up the pieces in silence over the coming months and years. I understand the isolation, the lack of intellectual stimulation; how you lost the sensual and sexual self you once were before your anatomy ceased to be simply your own and became first a home and then the sustenance for fragile new life. I understand how desperately you might want to escape and return to those days of luxurious baths, quiet dinners, good books and uninterrupted conversations. I know you love your children - and I know there are moments when something rises up in you that feels like rage, fear or despair when you remember who you once were and wonder who you have yet to become.

We are the generation who is to have it all: career, family, a perfectly toned body, a whiter-than-white smile, a wrinkle-free complexion, a Land Rover in the driveway, a golden retriever, an incredible marriage, wonderful friendships and, of course, picture-perfect children. These are the bald-faced lies we are fed by the media and television about modern motherhood.

The reality often is something more along the lines of: it's been days since you had a shower, you can't find the keys to your mini van – again! - and the dog just barfed on the carpet. After wiping up the mess and re-arranging a throw rug, you show up at school, late again with all your kids in tow and paste a smile on your face in case someone is looking. Somehow, you get through your day with the help of a pot of coffee, a bag of cookies; chopping lots of onions so that you don't have to explain your tears at dinnertime. You fall into bed exhausted, carefully avoiding your husband because he had 'that look in his eye' and you try to imagine how on earth you can get up tomorrow and do it all over again – only to have that thought interrupted by the baby who now is awake and ready to nurse, then your toddler falls out of bed and just as you are about to stumble back to bed, your oldest child has a crisis of confidence about his school play tomorrow and needs a 3:00 AM pep talk. Tomorrow ... damn it! Tomorrow is here and you are about to do it all over again, with only four broken hours of sleep to fuel you. I ask you; who among us wouldn't be pissed? I sure have been.

Choice by Choice

Motherhood, parenting – it's an intense, relentless, 24/7 process when children are young. I often found myself numbly going from one necessary task to the next while feeling completely disconnected from my own needs until I would reach a physical or emotional crisis that would force me to refocus on myself, if only briefly. One of my key discoveries after WEL-Systems has been how to stay connected to everything that is moving inside me so that I am not consumed by it. I am not immune to those moments of feeling utterly overwhelmed; however, I know things now that I didn't before. I trust my body to process in the span of a breath or two, all the energy and information in flow so I am resourceful for my children and myself.

I don't judge myself against a standard of 'normal' - I trust the genius and opportunity for discovery that stems from my imperfection. I know I have a choice about every step I take. Sometimes, it is as simple as choosing to stop long enough to have a drink of water or use the bathroom. There have been days when remembering to make those choices, moment to moment, was what kept me connected to my self. I used to ask myself – out loud – "what do I need right now"?

Other times, I have made the choice to lower the standards I set for myself that were unrealistic and based on an idealized notion of what a stay-at-home mom should be doing. When I was a working mom, I had a different set of standards for myself that were more flexible and reflected my self-worth as a financial contributor in our home. When I had my next two children and chose to stay at home, I really upped the ante on what I believed was expected of me. Not having an income threatened my sense of value. I felt like a freeloader and would burn with guilt when I wanted to buy things for myself. To justify it, I would set my standards even higher.

I was always adjusting myself to serve those around me. After having my body shift to accommodate my children during pregnancy, I found myself continuing to bend and flex after they were born. I recall leaving a family gathering one Christmas Day, choosing to come home to soothe a very fussy baby while the rest of my family remained at the celebration. I finally got him settled and asleep only to find myself kneeling to pick up an entire bin of Lego that my son and husband had dumped in the middle of the floor... and simply going to pieces, myself. This was NOT what I signed up for! Tired, overwhelmed, isolated and in servitude – I was filled with resentment and regret for how I had sold myself out.

Thankfully, I knew I could make different choices. I trusted the energy in my body to find resolution - and it did within a very short period of time. I moved forward with new respect for the seduction of the roles we play in our family and the power they hold to unhinge us. I know many women who only discovered their power to choose a different way of living after many years of silent struggle, often having been labeled as depressed and diagnosed with illnesses like fibromyalgia and diabetes. I sat with them as they grieved for the lives they could have had; and cheered alongside them as they stood tall with purpose and stepped boldly into a life of their own design.

Redesign & Rebirth

When I chose to enter the WEL-Systems programs, I was looking for some way to redesign and balance my life as a new mom and business owner. I knew I had lost big chunks of myself and I was determined to find them again. I remember feeling absolutely starved for meaningful, intimate conversations. I remember feeling like I was already half-dead and just going through the motions of my life and wondering what went wrong. I thought that I had finally 'arrived' in my life – career, marriage, family – but where I had arrived was a barren, arid place; not the one on the brochure!

That first program was a leap of faith. I was investing time and money that I didn't feel I had to spare. Even more challenging, I was leaving my child and my business to spend time sorting myself out. This felt profoundly selfish and yet I knew that I had to do something drastic.

By the end of the first hour, I knew I had made the right choice! These were conversations that were deep, authentic and free of any judgments. There were no expectations that I had to meet, no one I had to care for. I didn't have to be an expert or defer to anyone else's expertise about MY life. I showed up in all my confusion only to realize that I was not alone, I was not broken or defective and that I already had everything I needed to create the life I wanted – I had just forgotten. Over the coming months, I took the time to invest in myself, remembering how to trust myself and rediscovering the things that I felt passionate about. Along the way, I became a CODE Model Coach™ and reconnected to my passion for writing.

By the time I had my second child, five years after my first, I was an entirely different woman. It was a pregnancy that I could revel in – when I wasn't throwing up! I was able to give myself what I had been unable to do the first time and that was time to sit and appreciate the miracle of this unexpected gift. Not surprisingly, labor was an intense affair but this time I had full and complete trust in my body. I had no fear and felt no resistance to the contractions, discovering how to ride them with my breath. I never required pain medication and moved through the process with minimal medical intervention thanks to my husband's willingness to sit and mindfully breathe with me through the hours it took for my second son to arrive. It was in complete contrast to my first birth experience. I felt as though a new part of me was born along with my son – a woman who no longer feared the power of her own body.

A short fourteen months later, I was given another unexpected gift - my third son was an even greater surprise. There were such large gaps between my first two children; I figured I had some time to mull over a third pregnancy. This child was the fulfillment of an intention I had held for a long time. I had wanted three children but didn't want to have another after I turned 40. These seemed mutually exclusive at the time however; life has a way of delivering our heart's desires in spite of our limited beliefs. Once again, labor was an incredibly different affair. I opted for an epidural so that I could sleep until it was time to push. It was a great choice, since it seems I have barely slept since his arrival nine months ago! - just before my 40th birthday. Once again, a part of me was born along with my child – a part that knows and trusts her power to creatively fulfill her intentions.

My life barely resembles what it was five years ago. It began to change quickly after my discoveries through WEL-Systems and it continues to speed ahead with incredible joy and intensity. My fire energy for the most part finds its expression through creativity. My sons are my most potent creative stimulus. I choose not to live in secrecy, perpetuating the myths of motherhood or allowing myself to be consumed by cultural expectations. My joy lies in writing about my life with my children and what they teach me. Together, we are fulfilling our potential.

Wake Up!

Potential and possibility are the birthright of each and every one of us. What we ache for is the ability to create and express ourselves in this world from the core of our authentic being. We stumble under the weight of cultural expectation and sell ourselves out as adults in our quest for security, only to watch that security evaporate before our eyes in our rapidly changing world. Our children deserve better. They need to know that they can create their world in a way that honors who they are as individuals; that it is a safe and abundant place. Many of us have lost sight of the vision of our future as we wander blindly through our lives, often in a state of numbness and disconnection, hoping it will be better tomorrow and doing nothing to make it so. What little we have done up until now hasn't worked and the evidence is all around us.

It's time! It's time to wake up to our potential to shape our world and to teach our children how to do the same. It's time to become a Guardian of the Vision and to claim your birthright of potential. Your unique potential may have been forgotten long ago but it lives on inside you. Wake up! - So that the children of this world remain connected to their birthright. Wake up! – And live the life you want to live instead of the one you feel you are stuck with. You deserve more and so do your children.

Anita Allen is a Physiotherapist, CODE Model Coach™, a writer/speaker and the mother of three amazing boys. She offers individual coaching, workshops and keynotes to those seeking to live as an expression of their full potential.

Anita has a special interest in working with mothers and those who wish to explore their creativity through writing. She writes regularly in her blog, ***motherlode***, and is currently working on a book, aptly titled, *"A Work In Progress"*.

TAKING OFF THE CLOAK

Naomi Irons-Hill

I have gotten REALLY honest with myself over the last nine months and I am about to become very honest with you. I believe we are guardians and parents at a choice point in life - and the time is NOW! We can either choose to awaken and reclaim our unique Spirit within, encouraging our children to keep their connection to the unique Self they were born with; or as a society we can continue being disconnected from ourselves, modelling this to our children so they too, disconnect from their individuality to fit into to society's definition of 'normal'.

I can speak to this from my own experience. I was disconnected for many years and began parenting my own children based on the external reference points of what was considered normal and acceptable - before I chose to awaken to myself. As I awakened, I began questioning the forces that shaped me and asked myself: who was I before I put on the cloak of cultural conditioning so that I might look like everyone else? Who could my children become if allowed to develop outside of the influences that had shaped me?

I began to parent for the potential of my children's uniqueness because I had broken the mold. I reclaimed my own potential. Allow me to share my journey back to rediscovering and reclaiming the unique expression of my Self; and from there, my discovery how to 'be' a parent as an expression of who I am, rather than simply 'doing' parenting.

I remember being an adventurous child with great intensity, curiosity and spunk. I would venture out of the house alone and unafraid at the age of two. My mother would find me out in the field, wrapped around the hind legs of our Draft horses. I did all the things I wanted to do and never questioned if I was doing the 'right' thing in society's eyes.

Then life happened! Along the way, I began to notice I was a unique individual and I could attract a lot of negative attention wanting what I wanted and speaking my mind. The intense, curious, spunky little girl that I was became unsafe to expose. I learned very quickly that if I said the things people wanted to hear and set high standards for myself, everyone was happy and I got what I wanted. Looking back now, I can see this was the point when I chose to disconnect from who I was in the world in order to fit in.

Years went by and I continued achieving the high standards I had set for myself. I had begun a successful business, married the love of my life and without delay, started a family. And yet, I did not feel fulfilled.

As time went on, I became more restless and less content 'performing' the roles of mother, wife and business owner / massage therapist. These roles were becoming exhausting! I began desperately seeking for something I thought to be missing in my life and yet, continued the search outside myself.

I had everything that, by society's standards, should make for the perfect life. I had begun a family of my own. I had a successful business and great friends. I was financially secure. I fed my family organically, did yoga and meditated. I was very organized and travelled on great trips. I had a wonderful home in the country. But in the quiet moments when I wasn't performing countless distractions in the various roles I played, I was secretly dying on the inside.

I continued to seek outside of myself in the form of conventional and alternative therapies with the hope that they could fix what was going on deep inside me. Nothing seemed to offer a permanent solution. Along the way, my body manifested many wake-up calls. I suffered, at one time or another, with TMJ, PMS, headaches, depression, anxiety and chronic reoccurring flu and colds. At the time, I thought the wake-up calls were cues to eat better, get more rest or take a vacation. I now know that this was energy and information my body was trying to process but I had yet to awaken to the messages and insights available by simply relaxing into what I was feeling.

My awakening moment presented with the birth of my daughter. She was born into this world with the intensity and spunk I had long forgotten. She became the invitation for this to once again awaken within me. When I began to awaken to my authentic spirit, the flood gates opened for me. It felt like 25 years of unclaimed experiences were moving through my body all at once! A huge wave of powerful emotion flooded my entire body.

It was so intense, I had a hard time trying to suppress the sensations within my body. I was a new Mom with a 2 ½ year old and had a household and a business to run. Why would I want to move into these feelings of overwhelm, sadness and frustration? I had previously experienced what I thought was depression and I did not want to make that a part of my daily life again. I blamed how I felt on post pregnancy hormones, sleepless nights and the transition into having two children.

I ended up doing what I knew and believed to be right at the time; and moved away from what was trying to awaken in my body. I once again disconnected from my body which essentially disconnected me from my Self. Looking back now, I can see that once the body begins to awaken, it is like trying to put a lid back on something that is boiling over ... and it becomes a big mess!

I became a mess! I had so many sensations and emotions (energy and information) running through my body that I was trying to ignore. Trying desperately to stay disconnected from the emotions and sensations that were running through my body, I dove further into the 'role' of Mother and even farther away from myself.

I stayed at home with my two children for nine months, trying to distract myself from my inner turmoil by again setting increasingly higher standards in my life and the lives of my children. By the time I went back to work, I was beginning to question: what was 'wrong' with me? Why didn't I feel happy when from the outside it looked like I had a great life? I could no longer blame it on the pregnancy hormones or sleepless nights so I had to create new reasons why I was feeling so many sensations trying to move through my body. Maybe I was depressed. Maybe I was sick. Maybe I was ungrateful. Or maybe I was not meant to be here at all!

While all this was going on inside my body, I was trying to stop the flow of emotions within my children with discipline and distractions so they wouldn't become a constant trigger or reminder of what was moving in me. Every time they acted out or 'pushed my buttons', they would become the invitation to awaken what I was trying so hard to lock down within myself. Not wanting my floodgates to open, I tried desperately to suppress their expression, unaware of what I was doing to them.

I wanted what society encouraged so I parented for the outcome of well-mannered children that were praised for being smart, courteous and well behaved. As I parented my children, I taught them how to be noticed for the very thing that disconnected me from my Spirit 25 years ago: I taught them how to please others and become achievers. I was teaching and modelling to them that what others said was more important than what they had to say; and that by setting and reaching high standards for themselves, they would get what they wanted in life. I was on my way to teaching them how to cloak their individuality in order to conform and fit in.

Looking back now, I wonder why I thought I could foster happiness for my children using the same thinking and strategies which created my unhappiness. At the time, I didn't know how to do anything else. I longed to do it differently and knew I wanted to stop the frantic, time consuming search

Taking Off the Cloak

that kept turning up the same old information and dogma; all the same information in different guises that was available in the same old paradigm. Then one day, I followed an impulse I had in my body and signed up for the Decloaking experience offered through the WEL-Systems® Institute.

This program became the choice point for change a short nine months ago and I have yet to look back. I entered the WEL-Systems experiences and the choice to look under the heavy, dark cloak that surrounded me became available; and this time in a much different context, a different paradigm, than I had ever experienced before. I had spent years looking and searching for the right course, book, retreat or trainer. I was looking for someone else to give me the answers for fulfillment. When I came across WEL-Systems, I had no idea I could choose to look at the world differently. In that realization, everything in my life began to change.

I had originally signed up for the program to become a better mother and massage therapist but it was quickly evident to me that to change the way I carried out these roles in my life. I had to know who I was under the culturally conditioned roles/cloaks that for years had defined my very existence. I finally began to trust my body and the sensations that ran through it. This began the process of reconnection to the intensity, curiosity and spunk that was the essence of the real me, my Authentic Spirit.

I began to feel safe within the territory of my body and was able to relax into the emotions and information that tried to move so strongly in my body after my daughter was born. I came to learn that our bodies are organic bio-processors, designed to process this information; and that breathing and relaxing into what moves in the body is as complicated as it gets. It was wonderfully easy and very powerful! Years of culturally conditioned beliefs, attitudes and values simply vanished as I became more and more present to the Authentic

Spirit that was me, expressing through my body. I was awake for the first time in years and I was in the presence of others who were choosing to be awake as well.

When I returned home from the first program, I became very aware of the command-and-control parenting style I had used as a strategy with my own children. I had believed my children would fit into society with more ease if they were obedient and listened to those in "control". I had never questioned, until now, what happened to my children's voices as they listened to those outside themselves, allowing the truth of their experiences to be overridden by another person's version in order to be polite and be a "good child". It was the same thing that happened to my voice years ago: what I said on the inside did not match what I said on the outside and even worse, at times my voice completely disappeared. This was the life I was creating for my children, all in the name of "proper parenting" and "love".

Things began to change inside of me as I started questioning my beliefs that had been put in place through culturally conditioned dogma in my home, school, community, etc. As I have embarked on this journey to reclaim myself, I have begun to parent VERY differently. Before, I would be paralyzed with fear if my children or I were confronted with the experience of not fitting in. As time went on and I was able to let my body process the times that I was reprimanded for being 'Me', the fear then disappeared; and as a result, I no longer feared for my children when they were being themselves and possibly not fitting in. I was able to let my children be themselves in public with more ease knowing if someone had a problem with it, I would allow my children to speak what was true for them or that I could step in as an advocate for their voices if it came to that.

Furthermore, I now respect my children's individuality and I no longer need them to fit in so that I may feel comfortable. Allowing them to speak for themselves has created the space for very different conversations and awareness around our individuality within our family. I also now know when information (sensation/emotion) moves in me, it is about me - and when it moves in someone else, even in response to something I have said or done, it is about them.

I knew that if I could be myself and become the invitation within my family for a different conversation, the earth could shift beneath us and generations of cultural conditioning could simply disappear. It has become a ripple effect within my family. Nobody has been left untouched from my willingness to simply be me. This became a critical conversation with my Mother because for years, the two of us tip-toed around each other, afraid to set each other off by things we did or said. It created a wedge between us that neither one of us wanted but up until now, we didn't know how to have the conversation differently.

This is how history repeats itself. To paraphrase Einstein, we cannot solve a problem at the same level of thinking that created it. We have to learn how to have different conversations within our families or NOTHING is ever going to change! The one thing I know about changing the conversation is that until I first changed the conversation with myself, I could never have had it differently with anyone else.

This certainly proved to be the case with my mother; and this more than likely would have been the pattern that I would have recreated with my daughter. The Mother-Daughter relationship, in my eyes, can be one of the most damaging if we are not able to see past the roles we play to know that we are simply two human beings interacting with what we know and have been taught. Unless the conversation changes through our willingness to become open, clear, honest, and direct with ourselves and each other, we are going to keep recreating the same patterns/conversations for generations to come.

My Mom is Holly and I came to be able to 'see' her for the first time as a Spiritual Being expressing in a physical universe. She is very special to me and for a long time, I didn't know how to see past the role she played as 'mother'. As our relationship changes and moves away from past conversations and the stories attached to them, a new world of possibility has opened up for my relationship with her and my relationship with my children. I now let my family 'see' me and I no longer hide behind the roles of mother, daughter, wife, massage therapist or friend, afraid to expose the fact that I didn't know myself when I wasn't performing any of these roles. I am ME in the magnificence of my imperfection. It's a wonderful place to stand!

My acceptance of myself, without judgement, has made it easier to embrace the unique Authentic Spirits of my children, family and everyone that I meet. This is an important conversation for me because I believe if children were encouraged to remain fully connected to their individuality and have this nurtured, the world would be a much different place to 'be'. I have always known this but I was unable to encourage this within my children until I first became interested in awakening and reclaiming *my* individuality, that lay deeply buried under the cloak of culturally conditioned beliefs. Wearing that cloak and burying my individuality was once a protection from 'standing out' but it became the very thing that was killing me from the inside.

I am meant to stand out. My children are meant to stand out. You are meant to stand out! We are all unique individuals and to be unique we must stand out. We are meant to have what comes out of our mouth match how we feel inside - without fearing any repercussions.

Cultural conditioning allows us to feel safe by blending in to the scenery and substituting the voices of the collective for our own, placing us firmly in the box of 'acceptable' and divorcing us from our unique Authentic Spirit. I modelled 'being in the box' to my children for the first few years of their lives but I have now chosen to step out of the confining box I thought represented safety in my old belief system. I am done with blending in and expecting my children to blend in, for the sake of making their family members or someone else feel

Taking Off the Cloak

comfortable. I hope my children choose to be awake but I know it is now up to my children to go out into the world and choose for themselves.

We are not weak, broken, dysfunctional or crazy. We are geniuses that have created genius strategies in order to move through our world safely. What I didn't realize until now is I am safe and the strategies that were at one time genius in keeping me small do not apply to my life anymore. I sure don't want to teach these to my children. Although I may not have had a choice as a child being raised in an old paradigm, we now have new information available in a new paradigm. I have a choice about how I continue to live and by extension, how I choose to nurture my children and their potential.

Do you want to pass on to your children your fears, insecurities and discontent? If you do, just continue doing exactly what you are doing. If you don't, begin to get curious about what else is possible. Many of us believe that there is only one reality, one way to see the world. I invite you to consider the possibility that this is not the case.

A WEL-Systems perspective is what freed me from my cloak of old, ill-fitting identities, offering me a new way to interact with my children and my family. You can begin to do the same for yourself by allowing the sensations and emotions that your children trigger in you to become the invitation to awaken to the potential you carry deep within you, buried under years of cultural conditioning. Look into your children's eyes to see them and not your own reflection.

I am now awake. I can now see so many children who are awake but on the brink of going to sleep and disconnecting from who they are, as a unique signal in the world, because they want so desperately to fit in to their family; to feel safe, loved and accepted by the very people they look up to and call Mom and Dad. In order to offer them an alternative to disconnection, we must first awaken to our own potential.

My hope for this book is that it will spark your search inward, allowing you to reconnect with the unique Authentic Spirit that you are so that you are able to become the guardian of the potential your child, grandchild (or any other child!) carries as its birthright. I believe this very thing will redefine parenting as we know it. No more techniques, practices or dogma. Simply awakening to our own birthright of potential; and in doing so, creating the space for children to remain awake, allowing them to continue to marvel in their individuality!

Naomi Irons-Hill is a Registered Massage Therapist, Doula (in training), Yoga Instructor and CODE Model Coach™.

Naomi is the owner of Renew Massage Therapy Clinic and offers a wide variety of experiences. Her passion lies in facilitating unique experiences for individuals and groups seeking to discover a new way to 'be' along the path to their Authentic Self. She is very active in her own Self-Evolution and knows it is a never ending process.

THERE IS NO OTHER WAY

Amy McNaughton

Introduction

If it weren't for Louise LeBrun and the body of knowledge that she has created, I wouldn't have a true understanding of what the impact of being *honest, open, clear* and *direct* could have on a person's life.

The journey that I started with Louise through the WEL-Systems® Institute has been the most incredible thing that I have ever experienced in my life. With this body of knowledge, I have reclaimed my life; and because I have discovered who I am in the world, my daughter can now discover who she is, as well.

My search for new information and my willingness to consider something different means that my daughter also gets to choose what is meaningful for her, based on her own experiences, rather than something that I've told her that I was told, and so on. Life can become meaningless if we are only using the past as our reference point for living; or it can be a life full of meaning *if* we choose something different.

Honest

As I sit here about to engage in the process of sharing something that is so profoundly meaningful to me (not to mention very personal), I notice the sensory cues in my body. My chest starts to feel a little tight and then, that sensation moves up to my throat. My throat is the part of my body that carries information about choice. It is the conduit that gives voice to what I experience in my body, enabling it to be expressed to the outside world. I take a deep breath, exhale and with a sigh, I relax my body and allow the energy and information to flow. I know that this is exactly what it will take to engage in parenting differently.

I need to start by sharing with you what I discovered during a writing retreat in December 2006. My body started to shudder as I listened to another woman as she shared her experience of giving birth to her son and how sacred it was for her. My daughter was around nine at the time and what came into my awareness was that I had allowed myself to be consumed by the experience of being a mother. I realized that beyond being Meagan's mother, I had no idea who I was.

I had built my life based on the belief that you put your child first, always and without exception. Your child is your first priority and your needs aren't as important. Your needs can wait until your child is grown up. It's as though you have a life and in a moment you surrender who you are, to serve this small being. You do it without hesitation and know that in a breath, you would sacrifice your life for this 'tiny miracle'.

That willingness to surrender who you are and sacrifice your life for this new child, comes from so deep within the body that you don't question it. There's a 'knowing' that goes beyond what we know to be logical. That was my experience then and I wouldn't have done it any other way. Of course, I didn't know any other way then. However, what I do know now is that you can give to your child and still continue living without a sense of getting left behind or lost.

Looking back on my experience and hearing the experiences of other women, is it any wonder that so many women go through something referred to as postpartum depression?

Since the day Meagan was born, I have always been honest with her. Even when she was a baby and may not have been able to communicate with me verbally, I was honest with her. Children, even infants, can understand what we're saying.

There's a different vibration to being honest than there is to when we lie, and that is what I believe infants pick up on. Allow me to share the truth of my own experience, claiming where I was before my discoveries through WEL-Systems and how things have changed as a result. Not only have things changed, but I have a different understanding of how and why being honest with my daughter is so important to me. I am not here to judge my past and how I was parented. I am choosing to move forward in my life with new information; and with this knowledge, *I am able to choose to engage differently.*

I parented based on my own personal history because that is what I had as reference. Making choices based on my experiences of being parented, I did what I felt worked for me and when I remembered the things that I didn't feel worked for me as a child, I would then choose to do the opposite. Personally, I knew long before I got pregnant that I would not lie to my child because of my own experience of being lied to when I was a child. I remember being referred to as the 'emotional one' in my family. As a child, when you hear someone lying to you and they're denying it, it causes great pain in your body. Energy and information that defy words begin to move in your body and often, your only option is to push it down and keep it inside. Without fully understanding what is going on, you know that this is a 'safer' option than to argue with an adult. When a child knows that they're being lied to; and the adult stands there and blatantly continues to lie, it is the first step in teaching our children that lying is okay.

You may think, "Well, under the circumstances, I had no choice." We always have a choice. It's the choice to be honest or to lie. *It's that simple.*

Since I've made the choice to live from a WEL-Systems paradigm, I have a new perspective on honesty. Honesty, for me, is something very important with implications for our health and well-being. When what goes on inside the body doesn't align with what is being expressed, tissue changes and health issues develop. As long as my daughter is at an age when I'm responsible for her, I need to ask myself some very important questions. Am I willing to take on responsibility for teaching her to lie? No! Am I willing to take on responsibility for creating an environment that may create health issues for her? No!

I remember when my sister was sick and dying of cancer, Meagan was a little over two years old. I shared with her that Auntie Anne was dying. I also shared with her, to the best of my ability, what was physically going on and moving through Anne. I told her what cancer was and what chemotherapy was. I did whatever it took to offer Meagan a better understanding of what was taking place. So when Meagan saw Anne for the first time without hair on her head, eyelashes or eye brows; and noticed that her skin had developed a yellow tinge, Meagan did not react any differently to Anne because there were no surprises for her.

Our children can handle the truth. The question is, are we willing to deliver it? I did not stunt my daughter's growth by sharing the truth with her however, I did create a safe space for her so that she would not feel frightened by what she was seeing. Anne didn't look like she used to and yet Anne was still very present, and that is what Meagan knew - even as a child. I never made up stories because she was 'only' a child. I know that it's more devastating to a child to know and sense the truth in their own bodies, only to have the person that they love deny it by lying to them. Honesty is vital to a child's growth, both physically and mentally.

Meagan is twelve now and I know that she doesn't ever wonder if what is coming out of my mouth is true or not. While it has always been the case, at this age in particular I want her to be able to ask questions and have her know that I won't make up a story because of my own discomfort. How many times do our children's questions receive a haphazard response because we are uncomfortable answering their questions?

Open

I know for myself that it's important for me to create a safe space for openness. I chose to have openness between us because it's what I would have wanted for myself when I was a child. If I don't create it, where does my child go? If I'm not the safe, open space that she knows she can come to when her world is chaotic, where does she go? I need to know - as much as she needs to know - that she can come to me at any time and we can talk about what is going on in her life.

I create the environment where my child learns and experiences what it's like to be part of a family system. I'm responsible for her and I take it seriously. That doesn't mean that I take the back door and always put her first. It means that I stand tall in who I am in the world, allowing her to see that she gets to make the choices that are best for her.

Apart from 'raising children', we're sharing our own life experiences with another individual. That they are smaller in size does not, by any means, make them any less than we are. It's important for me to create a space that is honest and open because without that, there is no authentic communication going on. If I don't take time not only to listen to Meagan but to truly hear her, where will she go for someone to acknowledge her experiences and be with her without judging her?

At the age of twelve, many adults tell her that, "These are the best years of your life." Hmmm... funny... *she* doesn't feel that way! I remember when I was about to say something to her and she said, "Whatever you say, don't tell me that these are the best times of my life." I smiled; I wasn't going to say anything of the sort. Even though it may not seem like a big deal for me (given my age and life experiences), what she is moving through in her life is a big deal for her - and that's what matters.

For the most part, I listen and offer suggestions but her choices have to be hers. She needs to be comfortable with the choices that she makes. There are times when we have chats and she comes to a decision that I wouldn't make however, *I am not her.* We learn from our own experiences, not by someone else's experiences. For every choice we make, there is an outcome. Sometimes, the outcome isn't exactly what we would have liked. Those moments - when there is an outcome that she may find difficult to accept - are the moments when I need to know that we have an honest, open, clear and direct relationship so that she can come to me and she can open up without fear of being judged or reprimanded.

Sometimes, the safe space that I create for her is as simple as asking her a question. "What do you need from me right now?" Just a couple of weeks ago, she was in tears and I asked her the question and she said, "I don't know." Another question, "Why are you crying?" "I don't know." I wasn't going to dispute that she didn't know why she was crying or didn't know what she needed at that point and so, I chose to lay beside her on her bed and simply be there. Sometimes, there are simply no words to express what is going on in our bodies, so why would I make her search for an answer that may not be there at that point? Why would I put her in a position of questioning her own body responses, making her think that something was wrong with her?

As I lay beside her, she opened up and shared with me what was going on; and it just so happened that it had to do with me. Hmmm! Yep, I'm human, too; and I too, make choices that I don't like the outcome of. That day was one of them. I was reminded through my daughter's openness that it's important to pay attention to what is coming out of my mouth. Funny that we 'preach' to our children to watch what they're saying and yet, as an adult, it's totally acceptable to say whatever you please. "You can say whatever you want when you're forty," is my husband's favorite expression. Needless to say, my husband and I parent differently. That's okay too because Meagan gets to choose what works for her and what doesn't, based on her own experiences.

Clear

I don't know how many times I've heard my husband say, "I don't read minds." Well, neither do most of us – and yet sometimes, we seem to speak in code which isn't only frustrating for the other person but also for ourselves. I have to say that this was a big learning experience for me when I started my journey through WEL-Systems.

"What do you mean by 'ask for what you want'?" It seemed like a totally new concept for me – and yet, it's so simple: if I'm going to be honest and open, then hey! – why not start being clear? I know that this has been a huge discovery for me when it comes to parenting.

Considering that I parented Meagan based only on what I had known before, she has had at least nine years of hearing me speak in code. This is not the case anymore. The three of us are very clear now, when we're speaking to each other, so we no longer have to figure out what the other one is trying to say. I know that if I want Meagan to do something and I ask her clearly, she usually does it right away. My way of moving through the world isn't about, "Do what I say and not what I do," it's about being honest, open, clear and direct. There truly is no other way.

No beating around the bushes. No requests that leave out the details which may be required to complete a task. I used to get frustrated when I'd ask her to clean her room. Well, she has a totally different perspective than I do when it comes to what cleaning a room means. So now I'm very clear and give the details of what *I'm looking for*. The same holds true for Meagan. What I find is that there is less frustration and annoyance that takes place in our home because there's clarity in our communication now, that didn't exist before. If Meagan wants something, she asks without making up a story around it.

'Story-telling' is something else that stopped. Stories are about the 'he said, she said' of life and omit the person talking. In a family, if we engage in telling stories, no one ever has to claim responsibility for anything. It's quite genius, and I know of no better way than story-telling to create chaos in our lives. I've always wanted my child to be honest, open, clear and direct but how is she going to learn if I don't model it for her? Not living as an example or expression of what I am teaching her, is a double standard – not to mention, very confusing.

When Meagan asks why I have responded 'no' to a request, my answer is never "Because I said so." Sometimes there is a clear cut 'no' and sometimes I honestly can't give her an answer as to why. However, I tell her that I honestly don't know - that it just doesn't feel right. Following my gut instinct has never failed me. She understands where I'm coming from and 'trusts' that I simply won't make up a 'false' story just to manipulate her. Now when I say 'no', there is no feeling of guilt attached to it so there is no need to apologize for my answer. There's an understanding that the answer is based on a sensory cue in my body (a gut instinct... heart-felt), so I don't question those impulses in my body when they're so strong and I know that the body, unlike the intellect, is incapable of lying.

As clear as I may be about things, I also have the right to change my mind. Nothing is ever set in stone. Everything that I write above applies to everyone in our home – including Meagan. She is capable of saying 'no' and of changing her mind. I don't throw a 'hissy fit' when she says, *"No, not right now. I don't really feel like doing that."* All of this creates opportunity to engage in conversation with my daughter. I could look at it as her being defiant or I can consider it as her choice to do what is meaningful for her and create a conversation around it. By choosing to have a conversation, I can discover more about my daughter and what she is experiencing, rather than getting angry. The only way for me to know what is true for her is by simply asking. I can't possibly know that until I choose to engage with her – to do otherwise *would be to make up a story.*

Direct

Being direct is so simple for me now. I used to worry that I wasn't being a good mother when I spoke directly. I felt like I had to soften my words. I always say that it's all in the 'delivery.' If I speak with conviction, trusting my body to take the lead, then I know what's coming out of my mouth is right for me. This allows me to be honest, open, clear and direct without being harsh or abrasive in the delivery. If I chose to speak from habit based on my old perceptions, I may have been waving my finger - other hand on my hip - with a sense of, "I'm the mother and you don't get to question anything I say."

I believe that our children would appreciate it if we always chose to be direct without speaking in 'code' or 'beating around the bushes' so everyone knows exactly where they stand; and there's absolutely no guessing game taking place. When I speak with conviction, Meagan can sense that what I'm saying is exactly what is true for me in that moment. Rarely does she question what I say. Before, when I would say something, it was kind of…well… wishy-washy. When something comes out of my mouth that isn't coming from my gut instinct, it really does sound like a story. Meagan knows a story when she hears one. Stories are unclear and that is when she questions what is coming out of my mouth. Who could blame her?

Direct happens naturally when you're honest, open and clear. There's nothing to figure out or to soften when I trust my internal cues.

There Is No Other Way

I'm pretty sure that we all want our children to grow up and be 'respectful adults.' My question is: what are we doing and who are we 'being' in their presence, to show or model for them what respectful actually is? How are we choosing to speak to each other in our homes? Do we speak differently to others when we're not at home? It's time for us to really get honest with ourselves and reflect upon our own up-bringing and how we were parented. Did people see your family as one way in the community and did you experience the total opposite in your home? We need to get honest and ask ourselves the same questions about the home environments that we're creating for our children.

Louise LeBrun used a terminology that I truly love. **RIG**[1]... **R**espect – **I**ntegrity – **G**enerosity of Spirit. It's beautiful and is a wonderful 'notion,' however if it remains a 'notion,' it isn't something being experienced in the body nor is it a living expression of who we are. I share with you that this is the way that I choose to live my life. I have much **RIG** for many people in my life and it wasn't until I allowed myself to experience it in my life for 'myself,' that I was able to feel it towards others. We cannot give our children what we haven't got. If we don't RIG ourselves, how can we teach our children to RIG themselves or anyone else? We cannot teach what we, ourselves, do not understand.

If you're a mother reading this book and wondering how you can begin to make a difference in your home, then I invite you to ask yourself a few questions.

> **Do you remember who you are outside of being a mother, wife, daughter?**
>
> **When was the last time that you chose yourself, first?**
>
> **Do you invest in yourself because you *know* you're worth it?**

Believe it or not, these are crucial questions and I answer "Yes!" to all of them, now. It wasn't all that long ago that I would have looked at these questions and considered them

---

[1] "RIGing: A Powerful Alternative to Love" - Louise LeBrun; *Emerging Futures blog*, December 11, 2008; LouiseLeBrun.wordpress.com

to be outrageous or ridiculous. Now I have a different understanding of what these questions mean for me. If I don't answer 'yes' to these questions, what am I teaching my child? Possibly, to put everyone first before my own personal needs or wants? If that is the case, then there's a great chance that I will experience lots of annoyance and frustration because I'm not following the impulses (gut feeling – instinct – heart), in my body. We've been taught that the answers are outside of us for what we're experiencing inside of us. The answer to who we are is inside of us waiting to get out and be heard - if we dare let it. We can access the answers, along with other wisdom by trusting the cues in our bodies.

I believe that women/mothers are the key to creating the future that we want to see for our children. I also know that in order to create this, we must wake up, speak up, speak out and be heard. As parent, we need to lead by example. If we live life and recognize that everything that we go through is nothing more than an experience, without judging it as good or bad, then we move forward – trusting that in the next breath, we get to choose differently and so do our children.

I know that it's important for me to remember that I can't fully 'know' what my daughter is experiencing. Even though her experience may be similar to one that I went through when I was younger, her experience is unique to her and is very real. Too often, we use words that pretty much tell our children to 'put up – shut up – suck it up,' ignoring the chaos that is going on in their bodies. I'm happy to say that I don't give Meagan any words of advice anymore but I do offer some suggestions; and she gets to choose the ones that are right for her. In this way, I can acknowledge the truth of her experience with respect, while teaching her to trust herself.

I believe that we need to create a safe environment for ourselves and our children so that we may consider a different way of moving through our world. If we keep on repeating the past, we will end up in the exact same place. Changing any outcome requires that we engage – engage – engage, despite what others have to say about our choices. Someone has to go first.

I chose to go first in my life. Are you willing to be the first in yours?

Amy McNaughton is a CODE Model Coach™, Reiki Master and Registered Nutritionist. Her compassion and desire to create are the driving forces in her own life and in her work with others.

Amy creates a safe space for others to consider their lives differently: freeing themselves of self-imposed limitations so that they may discover how to reclaim a meaningful life. She encourages you to get in touch with her if you're interested in discovering what else is possible for you in your life as a parent; and first and foremost as an individual looking for something more.

ONE MAN'S EXPERIENCE
Ray Landry

Your children are not your children.
They are the sons and daughters of Life's longing for itself.
They come through you but not from you,
And though they are with you yet they belong not to you"…
Khalil Gibran

I have the privilege and am taking on the responsibility of writing a chapter in this book on parenting from my perspective as a man, a father and as my parents' child. I have no illusion that my experience will speak to, or can include, the experiences of all men who've become fathers; and even less to those who've had children and have never been involved in their lives. Yet, I have a sense that many of the experiences we have are common to us all and similar, at least on the surface, in that we have been handed down a very limiting and narrow view of what it is to be a father, a dad, a man, spawned by the dawning of the industrial age some 130 years ago and the supposed age of enlightenment.

I am grateful for this opportunity to add my voice to the clear and resonating voices of the women who lend their genius to these pages. I believe that in a time when so many families are experiencing the brunt of history repeating itself (and cracking under the immense pressure), there is still a unique, equal, and important role for me to play - as a man - in the evolution of the human species and in changing the present day unfolding of that history. Today, I choose to play my part in shaping my world not by default; not by simply claiming what has been handed down to me from generation after generation of patriarchal influence; not by designated roles or prefabricated notions of maleness, fatherhood, husbandry, being the "boss" or leader, but by <u>intention</u>. Only with great clarity about how I have been shaped and who I have become, can I stand in the present and claim my ability to choose, from moment to moment, to create a life that is meaningful to me and better for my children.

This is not an advice column or a "how to" guide (you might have deduced that from other chapters in this book!). I have no wish or will to tell others how to live. Rather, it is an invitation to reconsider all you've known before this moment, about yourself; and to know that the person you've become is key to how you play or perform your role as parent. It is an invitation to consider if you have ever found the tools to transcend those things that keep holding you back; that keep you feeling small or wounded. Because if you haven't, those things will show up when you're playing dad!

I offer to you, the reader, my experience of parenting in a new paradigm; of seeing through a lens that has offered me that gift of clarity and a limitless opportunity to discover what is possible for me as a parent, a father and a man that is very different from my experiences of those concepts growing up. I have come to know, through the lens of the WEL-Systems® perspective, that how I play the role of father and any other role I take on, is inextricable from who I hold myself to be as a human being. In other words, if I continue to hold within me notions, concepts or beliefs that limit the scope of what's possible for me to do and who I can be, I will never be able to move out of that context to allow for me to be a different or better parent…until I pay attention. I must raise my awareness to those things within me that I can then choose to change, should I want to. Do not seek wisdom in what follows but be the witness to an abbreviated description of my experience; and in that witnessing, come to reflect on your own.

> *"Wallowing in the past may be good literature. As wisdom, it's hopeless."*.　　　　*Aldous Huxley*

My experience of fatherhood, oddly enough, matches my experience as the person that I am... that I had been... both in quality and quantity. The joy I would experience in the early days of fatherhood was tempered by the anxiety of doing the next thing wrong; of running habits and reactions I could not and did not know how to control or change. The joy I experience now is a permanent fixture. The anxious moments and repetitions of old habits and reactions, are few.

The birth of my daughter is the most poignant example of my early experiences as a father. At the moment of her coming into this world, I was both exhilarated and overwhelmed. I stood in the most joyous moment of my life, bathed in sheer horror at realizing the awesomeness of what I had been gifted; along with the dreadful feeling of solitude that it was all my responsibility to make good on this life I had co-created. I basically continued from that point in the biggest guessing game of my life, being too self conscious to ask for help and too stubborn to admit I hadn't a clue what to do next. I kept moving from awesome joy to overwhelming fear and stress, depending on the demands of the moments at hand.

I can remember only one conversation between my spouse and I that had to do with how scary it was to be a parent. I can only assume that she must have felt those fears too! Much of the world of assumptions and expectations of her, as a mother, must have been overwhelming at times, if not all the time. What's clear to me now is that both of us argued over what to do, how to do it and when to do it, out of our so-called instincts and experience. And what experience could we be drawing from? We had never been parents! We were baptized by fire, like every parent has been since the dawn of existence.

We had only imagined what it could be like, perhaps thinking that having been a child was enough to qualify us as parents; or maybe having read a book or two on the subject could possibly prepare us to deal with the feelings that come up at four in the morning when already sleep deprived. Then, the only experience I could really be drawing from was what I had learned, consciously or unconsciously, from how I was brought up and how I had internalized that experience.

What was it that showed up in my words and in my behavior, every time? What was inside me! Most of it I was unaware of until it showed up, sometimes in a spanking, sometimes in a loud scream, other times in man-handling the child to move them to a controlled setting to "manage" their behavior; and almost always, my efforts were a reactionary, thoughtless running of habits and programming.

There was a time, a little over a decade ago, when I held a strong belief that I had failed at Life. I had failed as a husband, even worse as a father, and had no clue what it meant to be a man outside of those 'god given' roles. To me, those 'roles' defined me as a person, as a human being. I was confused, to say the least. I judged myself harshly. I was in my mid-thirties and my so-called life was crashing down around me. These and other conditions drove me into a deep depression that I tried to resolve with alcohol and avoidance. It didn't help matters that there was a flow of seething anger and pain burning deep within my psyche that exacerbated the rest. And through all this, I worked hard at keeping 'it' all together. When I failed at that, I became suicidal and fell into a slow downward spiral that had me planning my own demise.

I was my parents' son! That is to say, without judgment or condemnation, that all of my life to that point was lived in my own personal history. The concepts and beliefs, values and attitudes that had been passed down to me and/or that I had interpreted and accepted to be 'true' up to that point in time were "driving my bus". I had not been made aware of and so could not choose anything different for myself, at that time. I was a product of, and living the consequences of, being unconscious. I could only pay attention to the experiences I had had and not to how those experiences came to be; even less, how I could change my thoughts about them.

What I know today is that somewhere in all of that chaos, the entelechy (life-force) within me told me that this didn't make sense. This was not really how it was supposed to be. There was an awareness of the slightest glimmer of an as-yet unidentifiable possibility that life could indeed be different. When I could not make sense of things not making sense, I attempted to end my life.

By the grace of the god-force within me; and the helping and capable hands of some of Ontario's finest psychiatric doctors, nurses and facilities, I made it to the point of "stabilization". That meant that I was well enough to leave the hospital. By no means had I earned a certificate in knowing how to live! By this time, I had quit a well-paying job, moved back "home" and been separated from my wife.

I recall hooking back into life and having a clear sense that there was nothing on which to ground myself. I felt like the proverbial rug had been pulled from under my feet! I was left with no solid ground to walk on, and no model for living that made sense to me or motivated me to engage Life in any meaningful way. I felt unsafe and unsure all the time. After a year of dabbling at playing well-enough, I crashed again.

I knew enough this time to check myself in and make any excuse to be safe, from myself! My "safety switch" or only point of reference and joy at the time were my children. I was fragile. I thought that if I could not stand myself or love myself enough, that I could focus on the greatest loves of my life as a tenuous hold from slipping further down the path of depression. Only in my second year of laying low and recovering did I start noticing possibilities for myself.

I started noticing that my parents weren't there for me; that if I was going to 'make it', I had to start taking on the responsibility of living my own life - one that was different from the perceived expectations of society and family. I needed to find <u>my</u> way. What I came to realize was that I needed to know myself and see myself and the world through a new set of eyes. The pair of glasses that were handed down to me were distorted with other people's opinions and tainted with other people's pain, limitations and rules that no longer worked or made sense to me. It was not lost on me that through this hellish time, I could not be fully present for my children. I was emotionally unavailable, despite my best efforts to play 'dad'. To this day, there are blocks of time and events in those two years of their lives that I cannot recall. If there is one lesson that continues to resonate with me from this experience, it is this: that if I am not present to myself – my thoughts, my beliefs, my habits, my patterns, my attitudes – I cannot be fully present to others around me, including my children.

> *"It takes courage to grow up and turn out to be who you really are."* – e.e. cummings

I sought out the 'what else' that could be out there! In that journey, I was fortunate to find work in a place where a whole other worldview was being expressed in an Aboriginal community. I found soon after that even with the promise within that Aboriginal worldview, there was much shame mixed in with the humor and pride; and what seemed to be an even deeper history of intergenerational trauma and pain than that which I had experienced.

I sought ways that allowed me to do my work as a counselor that would allow the people there to feel safe in telling, or not telling, their stories and still find healing. That search eventually led me to the WEL-Systems Institute and Quantum TLC ™. In

One Man's Experience

that 'new paradigm', and its many models and mechanisms for understanding and re-discovering myself, my personal growth and expansion accelerated.

I've learned to relax into the experience of parenting and its uncertainties. Beyond those moments when I was clueless and still thought I knew best; beyond the fear of getting it wrong as a parent, I've learned to trust whatever presents itself from deep within me instead of allowing my automated reactions or set of unquestioned 'rules of life' to show up and rule the moment. I know today, that I am not the parent, nor the father or dad of my children's early days.

I know that where I used to subscribe to concepts of disciplining/punishing/owning/controlling 'my' children, I no longer do. Instead, those concepts have been replaced by an awareness - a fully present awareness! - that allows me to notice my 'conditioning' and then to choose my words and my actions, more often in a way that contributes to a deepening connection with those with whom I have been blessed to grow. I have become more of a facilitator... a guide... an observer of their innate genius; of their curiosity and creativity. I marvel at their ability to do just fine without my having to intervene or control their actions, activities and thoughts. The all-encompassing love that I experience with them, through them and for them is only possible because I am more available to receive it, sense it and claim it for myself.

My experience has taught me that I need to act with clarity and intention about what it is that I want to produce. There are too many distractions and other "interesting-yet-not-so-important" things to pull my attention away from my engaging fully as a parent. And through the last decade or so, I have come to know that nowhere is it more potent or possible for change to occur than within me!

It is easy to embrace the notion that "our children are our future". It is an indelible truth. It is like saying water is wet. What I have observed and experienced though, is that there are underlying assumptions about how they get to "be our future" and "who" they will be when they get there. Therein lies the risk of history repeating itself and stunting the growth of an already oppressed "product of humanity". The strategy of doing our best and letting the chips fall where they may just won't cut it, if we are to create a world where human beings flourish exponentially and freely.

How does one create the necessary conditions for the next generation to grow healthy, strong, bright, happy? By owning one's own experience in the present, so as not to force it, unaware, onto others. Nowhere in my experience have I been introduced to a universal "How to" manual on being a Dad. Although I clearly remember wishing, sometimes begging for someone to tell me how this thing called fatherhood is done, it seemed no one could answer that question.

Where we have held to the concept that "If we don't remember our history, we are doomed to repeat it", we now have much evidence that remembering it has not been the catalyst to truly evolving or to creating something new. Our history books are filled with bloodletting and wars; our present day is filled with bloodletting and wars. What have we learned? Remembering cannot be the key to change. We cannot focus on the "lessons" of the past and think that our future will be better. The only point in time we need, and indeed, the only point in time we do have access to, is this moment, this time, the present. Only at this crucial point can we influence the next part of our children's lives! What power we have! What an opportunity to gift ourselves and our children – the present.

So I ask you: "Is it possible for you to notice; to raise your awareness to the fact that from this moment on, you can actually do anything and become whomever you choose to be as a parent, a father, a dad, a man?!" Letting go of the limitations/rules/boundaries that were set from sources outside of you, that you might choose from an infinite source inside of you, the ways and means of moving forward that honors that truth within; that reclaims the intelligence that lies deep inside you that you might know that you are moving in the flow of your intention and purpose for living!

Maybe the only thing that is standing in your way is the depth of your awareness about the content of your experience as a child and how it continues to shape you to this day. Choosing, from that awareness, the things that are most useful in shaping my life and that of the children I have the privilege to share my life with, is the ultimate expression of freedom.

> *"The secret of dealing successfully with a child is not to be its parent."* Mell Lazarus

I have come to know myself to be from a source of infinite energy and love that was expressed through the actions of my parents' joining. I did not belong to them. They were the custodians of my early life, my potential; the guardians of my birthright to be the expression that I have become. I am clear that they (as I and everyone else I know) did the best they could with what they knew, when they knew it. It took me a long time to get over the limitations of their knowledge and to free myself from the long-standing traditions of adults who become parents before they gain an awareness of how they, themselves, have been shaped. It has taken me a long time to move beyond the lessons of the past to stand where and how I stand today.

I am mindful today, that I express myself more along the lines of the human being that I am rather than through any role that I play whether that be as a dad, a partner, a friend, a musician, an artist, a counselor. For me, it is only through that expression that I can join; and that I can invite my children and others to sit equally in the circle of life as an individual, each in our creativity and genius. As I see – through eyes that are curious, full of wonder, in awe of life manifesting through those who grace my path in the way they do – I continue to claim my place in my universe and to be the invitation for my children to claim theirs. My life is filled with joy! And in all that I am and am becoming, I am blessed.

Ray Landry, Owner/Operator of *Self Power Consulting...Connect... Engage...Evolve!* is a WEL-Systems Catalyst and CODE Model Coach™. A father to a 20 year old daughter and 15 year old son, he has worked in the fields of health and social services for over 24 years; as an administrator, a teacher, substance abuse counselor and mental health professional.

Ray expresses his passion for human development and spiritual growth through public speaking forums and individual Life-coaching and consulting services. His creative spirit is expressed through music, artistry, and writing.

NO MORE DANCING AROUND

Marie Smith

There would have been a time, not so long ago, when I would have hesitated to share my story. I would have chosen instead to silence myself and to dance around the topic for fear that it would adversely affect my husband and my son. I love them both dearly - and I love myself enough now that I am willing to openly share my experience of violence in my home. I am making a choice to live a larger and more expansive life. I know there is much more for me to discover about parenting and that by being willing to share the truth of my experience, without judgment or blame, I will be opening the door to more meaningful conversations with my husband and son. I am willing to expose what I believe is prevalent in many households - violence - and in doing so, I hope that it will bring an end to the cycle in my family and beyond.

Since I began participating in programs offered at the WEL-Systems® Institute three years ago, my life has profoundly changed and expanded. When I think of an analogy of how I used to live life, it was like climbing a mountain, always trying to climb harder and faster but never reaching the top. I felt exhausted, discouraged, overwhelmed and stuck. In the new context I discovered through WEL-Systems, I have simply moved around the mountain with "effortless effort" by making choices with new information and trusting my body to digest old experiences and offer me new insights. It was like peeling off the layers of an onion, each layer offering me a larger and more meaningful life, bringing me into deeper connection with who I really am.

I know our children learn through what we model. In my case, I modeled how to dance around violence and how to dance around the edges of my life. There is no point to beating myself up anymore, as I did the best I could with what I knew at the time. Now, I continue to embrace my confusion, chaos and uncertainty with welcoming arms, allowing myself to breathe fully into what the moment brings and savoring my discoveries.

I have been married for 26 years and for 23 of those years, we were a military family. We have a son who is now a young adult and has left home to begin the next phase of his life. Throughout our marriage, we moved many times. Sometimes I would welcome the change; and over time, it became tiring. Each time, we would start over in a new community and I would find myself uprooted. Although there was a family resource centre and a network of other officers' wives, I became increasingly disconnected and isolated. This was compounded by the secret of the violence that I was living with.

Although we have never openly discussed it, I believe that my husband's life experiences have left him with what I would now call 'fire energy' in his body that has yet to be 'digested' and integrated. Fire energy is neither good nor bad - it is simply energy and information. In some cases, it might be labeled rage, fear or intensity; and in other expressions, it is passion and creativity. When it remains unresolved within the tissue of the body, it erupts like a volcano, releasing its pressure – until the next time. In our family the eruptions come in the form of verbal tirades; and often, my husband's barely-controlled rage is a frightening sight even though he has never physically harmed my son or me. When I was living in an old context of secrecy, all that was available was to struggle in silence to manage it – and that is what we did, each in our own way.

What I have since discovered through WEL-Systems is that when fire energy is relaxed into in the tissue of our body, it moves as sensory information (ripples, waves, heat, itchiness etc) which allows the body to process it quickly and easily, much like 'digesting' and 'metabolizing' the energy in a meal, but in this case what is being digested is old energy and information. However, many of us have never been taught how to trust our body to do this. Instead, we shut down what is actually a natural process and try to manage it.

Before I knew this, I managed my husband's fire energy by shutting down. I disconnected from my own fire energy, locking it in my body. I would attempt to make myself smaller and smaller in order to avoid becoming a trigger. I inserted myself between him and my son, doing my best to be a buffer. I experienced many moments where I felt 'spaced out' or had big gaps in my memories or in my conversations. They were all strategies I had developed, out of my awareness, to keep this a secret from others and to shut down the energy that was trying to move in my body as tears, fears, frustrations, anger and so on. In doing so, I began the dance.

It was a dance of silencing myself, not silencing myself; isolating myself, not isolating myself. I would turn in on myself, feeling uncertain about who I was. I found comfort in pouring everything I had into becoming a wonderful and engaging military wife. I invested myself in my husband's career and success, and in my son's well being. I remember talking to my sister over the phone, gasping, "I can't breathe in this marriage!" She suggested I do something for myself to create some 'breathing room'. It was a pivotal moment. I chose to start taking university courses – just for me! Unfortunately, it wasn't quite enough to fully reconnect me to who I was, deep inside.

Instead, I created my identity around being a 'strong' mother who did whatever was required to ensure the welfare of my son. I now recognize that being a 'perfect' mother is a myth. It is unattainable and yet so many of us buy into it. I did not see myself as a friend, sister, neighbor, wife, teacher or colleague – let alone 'Marie'! I was only focused on 'mother' as my identity and as a result, my world came crashing down when I became an 'empty nester'.

Because of my dance with isolation, I came to depend on my son as my support system. He is my only child and after each move, when everything around us was unfamiliar, we just had each other to rely on. It's not that my husband wasn't a capable or willing partner, but he was absent much of the time as he focused on his career. This, compounded by my desire not to trigger his outbursts, led me to depend on my son for conversations about the household, the finances and other things where I was seeking a sounding board. These were adult conversations that pushed him into a role that was beyond his years and became a foundation for his perception of what it is to be an adult male and a caretaker.

Not long ago, while in a WEL-Systems program, the term 'emotional incest' emerged in a conversation and I instantly felt the truth of it in my own body. I wept at the realization and allowed the energy and information to move through me; and as my body stabilized, an insight surfaced. What I couldn't see back then was that he was losing his connection to himself, at a young age, because of how I was interacting with him as his mother. I was incapable of seeing what was happening to him then because I was completely disconnected from myself. Without this information, we had marched on, each losing bits of ourselves, by ourselves. It was a dance of isolation and collusion.

Our dance of collusion reached its peak on the day of our move from what had been our family home for 10 years. We were leaving the Maritimes to move to Ottawa as my husband and I had chosen to leave the military for a job in the private sector. It had all happened quite quickly, leaving us little time to adjust or to spend much time in conversation with our son who was about to leave home to attend university out west – a dream he had been working toward for several years.

This was a huge change for all of us. Our posting in the Maritimes was one of our longest and it felt very much like home. My son was a young adult now and striking out on his own in a brand new place; and with little warning, he was to also be without the home base he had grown accustomed to as an anchor. My husband and I were about to become 'empty nesters' in a new city and province. The enormity of the change that was about to happen was overwhelming for me. I can only imagine what is was like for my son to be catapulted into a new life at university while losing the stability of our family home, all at once.

I recall a defining moment in our dance. The movers had packed everything into the moving van. My son sat on the empty living room floor and I flopped down beside him. My son turned to me and said, "This is not as hard as I thought it would be". I looked at him with relief, as we didn't have many opportunities to discuss this sudden upheaval with him, assuming that his excitement about university was all that mattered to him. Although he was telling me he was all right with the change, something in my body told me otherwise. I believe at this point, because it was the road of least resistance for me - and heaven knows that I was not capable of helping myself at that time, let alone my son - I colluded in the lie that we were both okay. "Yes", I replied. "Everything is fine", yet deep inside of me I was screaming a silent cry for help!

The cost of collusion kept me from speaking my own truth and collapsed the space for my son to express what was happening in his own body at that time. The intensity of both of our situations was pressing up against us. We did our dance of collusion - silently turning inward. That is when, I believe, we turned our backs to each other so we could both 'survive' the next leg of our respective journeys. At that time, I wasn't sure that either one of us wanted to continue.

My son left me to start his life but we were so entrenched in our dance that it must have been a huge burden for him to watch me slowly fall apart. He had lost so much. More than simply moving away to a new start at university, he was without a familiar home base to return to. He had lost connection to his friends and to familiar haunts. Returning 'home' to Ottawa felt more disorienting than life at university. Nothing was familiar and I believe he may have felt as though he had lost some part of himself without the familiar to help him define who he was. The slate had, for the most part, been wiped clean. He wanted to escape the chaos and confusion in his body but had nowhere to turn. I worried about his mental health under the weight of it all but I was incapable of reaching out at the time – I was still dealing with my own losses as a result of our move and his departure from home.

Without my son to define me as a 'mother', my identity collapsed and I collapsed with it. All of my self-worth was wrapped up in that identity. I was spiraling down into an emotional black hole. I became physically ill. Looking back, even though it wasn't a conscious thought, I wasn't even sure that I wanted to continue living because my life had no meaning at that point. I was so disconnected from who I was, having spent all those years defining myself through my role as a mother and living my life through my son.

The fire energy that I had so firmly locked down in my body as part of my dance with my husband was beginning to create disease as I struggled with Diabetes. I discovered that even though I had spent years nurturing others, I had no clue how to nurture myself. This was my dance with disease.

Since discovering a new perspective through WEL-Systems, I have come to see the information and the genius that was my disease. Once I made a choice to continue to engage in my life - even if it was unfamiliar territory - diabetes served as a wake-up call to take care of myself. I had to walk for exercise and I enjoyed it. I had to eat balanced meals and nourish my body in order to regulate my blood sugar. I got attention from the people around me as they ensured my blood sugar was being monitored. I began to get my health back and then began to enjoy a more meaningful and joyous way of life. As I recovered my health and reconnected to my Life, ending my dance with disease, I noticed that my son's life was changing, too.

Our way of relating to each other and the conversations we were able to have, expanded. I remember one day in particular, shortly after I had begun my journey back to 'me', that is a perfect example of this. We were text messaging using MSN. All the familiar triggers were absent as we chatted freely, moving without effort into a conversation in which neither of us was hiding. I remained deeply grounded and connected to myself as he shared a challenge he was experiencing. I asked my son, "What do you need right now to help you through this?" To my amazement, line after line marched onto the screen in a constant beat. It was his truth and he had never before revealed it with such depth or clarity.

Throughout all the years when I believed I was being the 'perfect' mother who had all the time in the world to listen, we had never had such a meaningful conversation. I was fully present and my son responded in the same way. I did not become lost in the face of his confusion, retreating and locking down whatever it called up in me. Instead, I was able to breathe and relax into the energy and information that was moving in me. The space opened up for my son to share and the dance was over.

It has become clear to me that in order to connect in a meaningful way with my son, or anyone else for that matter, I must be willing to honor my truth, my experience and what it is that is moving in me. When I relax my body, I trust it. I believe that my body never lies. As I breathe deeply and relax into the sensations that are in flow, my body 'digests' the information and then presents me with a new insight. At one time, I would have called sensations 'emotions' and had all kinds of judgments about them. Now, I know that it is simply energy and information that I feel. Relaxing into it expanded my life; pushing it down made me sick.

I no longer define myself through my role as a 'mother'; and in doing so, I have reclaimed my own potential. During a couple of recent flights, I was reminded by the safety demonstration how important it is to put on the oxygen mask yourself so that you are able to assist your children in an emergency. I know, now, that it is only by reclaiming my identity as 'Marie' that I can hope to offer the assistance and guardianship of the potential that belongs to my son. I cannot give what I haven't got.

I also know that in order to create the space for my husband and I to continue to grow together, I must declare that my dance with verbal violence is over. I have new information and there is another way for us to communicate where we both are connected to our own birthright of potential. In this case, neither of us needs to diminish who we are. We don't have to be defined by our past and can choose to step forward into our future as a couple in our new life that just happens to have an empty nest!

My life just keeps unfolding, as I declare each of my dances to be over. On occasion, I find myself dancing but now I know that it is a reminder to reconnect to myself. My disease does not define me. It simply is a cue to nurture myself and to relax my body in order to allow energy and information from old experiences to reach resolution. My voice continues to grow in strength and clarity as I declare my dances to be over. Secrecy and isolation are part of those old dances. In sharing my experiences – in sharing what has been true for me - I can now move forward boldly into the life I want to create for myself. I can let go of the parts of my life that affected my health and my relationships, and keep the parts that mean the most to me. Best of all, there will be no more dancing around the edges of my life! My dancing days are over and I am firmly standing my ground!

Marie Smith is a CODE Model Coach™ now living in Ottawa with her husband while her son is off exploring a meaningful life for himself. Rigorous about her own self growth, she brings much experience and safety for you to discover the "more" of who you can become.

A military wife of 23 years and mother of an only child, Marie's growth and evolution are a reflection of extensive travel, formal education and the 'school of hard knocks'. These have been her invitation to turn inward, rediscovering and reconnecting to the full measure of who she is. Marie's mobile practice, *Trust Your Self*, makes it possible for her to engage with others in a way that invites expression of the potential that we all innately know comes from within.

SEEING THROUGH A DIFFERENT LENS

Lucy Hensel

What I know now makes me really wish I could go back and relive the years when my two children were young. NOT because I loved that phase; not because Mothering was satisfying and stimulating for me, but because I would have seen my tiny children's innate perfection and potential. I would have known that my daughter and my son are god forces or energetic signals streaming through a human body and I would have protected their innocence and respected their higher Selves.

Even at sixty, it's not too late to look at my world differently. I say this with conviction because over the last three years I have learned of another way of understanding who and what we are as humans, and who our children are. My journey of discovery is a work-in-progress full of wonder, and my thoughts on who I am – Lucy, Mum, Granny - change, expand and develop with each insight and new experience of myself. As a result of my new-found shift in perspective, I move through the world differently. It's not that I have answers now but the questions I have been asking are fertile ground for movement and growth. The exciting part is the trek through uncharted territory discovering what 'more' there is in me and around me.

Until recently, I wasn't keenly aware of my 'more' although snippets of my own delight, exuberance and whimsy had leaked out occasionally – always to be stuffed back inside quickly before anyone might see it and make fun of it. My 'more' didn't mesh well with what I had told myself I could and should expect from myself and in my life. Now I'm willing to reveal all aspects of myself – to myself and others; and I'm ready to claim this inner force as mine and see what unfolds as I engage it as I live more fully. It is truly a new way of BEING for me and it has implications for how I engage with my family.

This shift is as if I've put a new filter on my camera lens – one that allows me to see my world in a new way. Or is it a leap? A shift seems too small! It's a BIG change. It's not that I understand my world more *clearly* but it's that in its mystery, my world is magical. Confusion and uncertainty are all part of creating space for 'more' and its magic to surface. I know now that my ability to create my world is powerful and that my enlivened awareness is crucial to who I am becoming.

I believe that I am an energetic force - a signal expressing though the device of my body. Had I known who and what I am forty years ago; had I been aware of and connected to what I am calling 'my signal' or my Higher Self, my children's lives would have been shaped by profoundly different influences. Our context for living would have been situated in the WEL-Systems® paradigm.

Within this paradigm and the context of this book, I willingly engage my thoughts about what I wish I had known then - without regret for what was and could have been - related specifically to my own two children when they were young and to my four granddaughters, now. I know however, that my new take on life will shape any interaction I will have with children, whether the child/grandchild is 'mine' or not. I hope to be a pesky thought virus that invites others to examine their existing views on what we are and how that relates to their relationship with any 'child' in their life.

Then And Now

Instead of a parenting model based on the WEL-Systems paradigm which considers the implications for human life that we can draw from the science of quantum biology and physics, my children experienced a way of growing up based on what I had experienced in my family and on their father's experience in his family. My worldview at the time held that the body is a machine to be maintained and 'fixed'; that the reference points that guide our actions and decisions are outside of us; and that the child is to be trained and educated. Our parents learned their parenting skills from their parents and the trail continues back over countless generations. Firmly entrenched in this belief system, my husband and I passed on our values to our children, including how to fit in, just as we had been taught. Their sense of individuality and their place in the world were firmly contained within the bounds of what we valued and considered normal or acceptable.

As parents, we were certain that we had done a good job of providing for our family's health and wellbeing and of creating a space in which our children could grow up just as we had - enjoying a safe and sane environment permeated by our inherited world view: our values, our beliefs, our hopes and our fears. I was a pleased and proud Mother. My children became well-mannered, well-educated and intelligent; and are 'successful' adults now. However, when I look back, I see patterns I would never want to repeat.

At this point in my journey of self discovery and heightened awareness of the choices I have made, I can pick out a few stories which might be relevant to other parents and grandparents. The context for my Mothering was not one of 'Mother as Guardian of a Vision' and was more one of 'Mother as Protector of the Status Quo'. I am not proud of that any more; and I'm seeing it for what it was and I'm claiming it as a part of the learning experience that is my life. I hope that my courage to claim my 'mistakes' and reveal my imperfections might encourage others to look at their lives and mindfully consider the powerful force that every family system is. My invitation is to look at the familiar through a different lens and to recognize our capacity to make new choices as new insights arise.

Now that I have fully embraced the concept that I am an energetic signal within a quantum biological device (my body), I can no longer see my children or my grandchildren as I used to. I believe each of us is an energetic signal; one that is sourced from the cosmic void where all consciousness resides and streams through a human body. Each of my children, each of my grandchildren is a unique, valuable and irreplaceable part of the sacred whole. Each of us is here on Earth as a piece of the universal puzzle, sacred spirits expressing as human beings. In this paradigm, my children are children under my guardianship until they can live independently of me. I have a responsibility to care for and protect them and to allow them to develop into their full potential. They are not 'mine' to shape, mold or homogenize.

The *vision* that I will be *guardian of* is one that honors the innate ability of all children to grow and to create meaningful lives. My job as a Mother is to make sure they survive infancy and childhood with these capacities unharmed; and to guard, to honor and to nurture their sense of self and their connection to their Self. Their potential, their ability to live full and meaningful lives is a treasure to safeguard and nourish. Their uniqueness is what this universe needs. To reshape, stifle or dilute their potential is harmful to the child and dangerous for the future of the species. My hope for our collective future lies in our children's and grandchildren's innate ability to choose wisely for themselves and the planet. We don't have any time to waste.

No More!

I certainly can't undo what I did as a mother and a grandmother. I can, however, choose to act differently now with reference points that are internal, based on who I am and what I know to be valid and meaningful for me in each moment. These choices arise constantly and they are mine to make. My decisions, made minute by minute, will affect me and those around me. I'm willing to take full responsibility now. Back then, I wasn't ready. I was living in a parenting paradigm where the guideposts were external; and the importance of fitting into my collective(s) and of carrying the torch of the accepted beliefs and behaviors of past generations was highly valued. I was disconnected from my inner Self. I was highly dependent on the approval and acceptance of others.

For years and years, I short-sold myself and my children by silencing myself. At the beginning, I wasn't at all aware of what I was doing. I see now, with the benefit of hindsight, that part of my parenting pattern - an unconscious strategy that I was using - was a dance I two-stepped through with my husband. Early on, we had agreed that it would be better if we would present ourselves as a team for our children so that we didn't allow conflicting or contradicting opinions to get aired in front of them. Often this meant that I acquiesced to his decisions and judgment, in silence. I was the dance partner who followed his lead and at the time, I thought it seemed like a graceful and appropriate performance.

As I think about it now, I am filled with dismay. The sense I have now of giving in; of not standing up for and voicing what I was thinking inside; of allowing persuasive coercion and command-and-control tactics to hold sway over me and my children, fills me with shame and anger. I can only imagine how confusing our behavior must have been for each of them. Children pick up vibrations naturally and ours must have been fraught with mixed messages.

While we appeared to be a unified parental team on the outside, I was riddled with unspoken concerns and doubts about our decisions. Resentment and smoldering disagreements remained inside me, undeclared. As the children grew a bit older, I became more aware of what I was creating. I increasingly felt the need to shelter them from rules that I saw as too strict, too demanding, too rigorous; and from the hurtful reprimands that I felt were harsher than was fair. I had become less willing to collude, yet I did not openly voice my objections to the patterns we were living. Now, I see what a dishonest and ultimately crazy-making atmosphere we had created – all with the best of intentions! Later, when the children were old enough to see or sense some of this, we were in such a well-established pattern of routine interaction and 'good behavior' that neither of them ever spoke up about these patterns. I do understand how it would have been difficult for them to contemplate speaking out – we were all trying hard to avoid confrontations; by then it was part of our established way of 'being a family'. Through our silences, compromises and collusion, we were individually and jointly perpetuating the myth of the happy, intact family. We were neither respecting ourselves nor each other.

Another important 'No more!' along the way of my personal journey has been the recognition of my fears and how they have shaped me and my family. I remember well the night when I first woke up to the fact that I had been afraid of my own daughter all her life. I was 59 by then and she was 38. That's a long time to hold fear in my body, especially fear of 'my own flesh and blood'. It felt like a bomb going off inside when I put a name to, and claimed, what I'd been allowing myself to feel all these years. The explosion actually felt like I'd walked onto a land mine. I was engulfed by chunks of regret, disgust and anger - at myself and about the precious years of a potentially honest and close relationship I'd squandered. It was difficult but I talked to my daughter about my awakening. It felt important to me to voice out loud to her what had shifted in me and to try to describe to her the resulting immense relief and expansion in the tissue of my body.

If I try to reconstruct the origins of my fear, I can come up with stories about how very young I was to take on the huge responsibility for another person's life; that I'd had zero experience with infants until she was born; that I felt inadequate; that I felt guilty that I was not enjoying 'mothering' more – and on and on. In fact, it doesn't really matter which explanations are most valid. What is important for me is to realize how limiting my beliefs had been and how I had let my fear of my daughter, and my fear of my responsibility to her and for her, determine my behavior and control our relationship for decades. By fearing and/or not trusting myself as a result of my disconnection from my Higher Self, I also feared those around me - even those to whom I'd given birth.

Today, I know that I have no need to continue that pattern; no further need to brace myself against myself and against others. None of us is to be feared. Each of us deserves respect – for our uniqueness, for the force that we are, for our sacredness in this universe. I really can allow myself to respect myself and others, and to hold myself and others with integrity and generosity of spirit! How empowering is that as a way of life! How much saner might it be for all children, all grandchildren if we adults were to embrace these notions as our birthrights? Imagine what parental guardianship of future generations could look like if this were to become normal and widespread!

Another 'Never again!' for me has been around my ability to turn a blind eye to a child's sense of hurt, outrage, anger – something I can also now recognize as an intergenerational issue because of a recent encounter with it during a visit with my daughter and her family. One evening, seemingly out of the blue, my eight-year old granddaughter totally ignored my presence as she joined us in the kitchen of their home. She did not return my cheery, welcoming "Hi ". While she interacted with all the others at the table, she would not look at me and proceeded to ignore me through the entire dinner. When I withdrew, feeling extremely hurt but not willing to let on that anything was getting to me, I approached her and asked if I could give her a goodnight kiss on the forehead and she refused to accept that gesture as well.

I left my family in the kitchen that evening with shame and embarrassment rushing through me, closely followed by rage and indignation; and they exploded in me with tears and childlike gasps and shudders. Many old hurts from my own youth moved through my body that evening in the privacy of my bedroom. The energy and information in flow was old and fierce. It was the pain of not being seen for who I was as a child. It was outrage about the disregard for my innate innocence, joy, playfulness, love and spontaneity. It was rage at my powerlessness as a child to stand up to the forces of disapproval and disappointment that kept me feeling cautious and fearful, always juggling the moods of the adults around me. As a child, I received a direct message through shame that I was unworthy. I kept my sense of unworthiness and shame locked deep inside of me along with my anger and outrage.

Being shunned by my young, vibrant eldest granddaughter with whom I had thought I had a warm relationship was a sudden and atrociously painful shock. The force of rejection by one family member has always been a really powerful deterrent for action in my life. One of my family's methods for ensuring compliance and performance was to threaten disappointment or to hint at exclusion. To see my granddaughter actually enact shunning made me aware of how these tacit methods of censure get handed down from one generation to the next – and in this case, with increasing intensity. To see that an eight-year-old was able to carry it off with style, while the rest of her family pretended nothing was wrong with the power-play we were carrying on over the dinner table, was an eye-opener.

As a result of this incident, I've begun to notice how many of these same parenting 'skills' I mindlessly repeated when I was a young mother. I wonder how much rage and hostility are in my two children's bodies now as they approach forty? I see my own anger and hostility reflected in my granddaughter's action. I also find myself curious about whether those were my own daughter's strong emotions, her silence an unspoken approval as she watched her daughter say to me what she has never voiced, herself.

Just as I have never been open and honest with my mother about the hurt, shame and fear of abandonment that I have carried inside me, my daughter and I have never talked about all the information (a.k.a. various emotions) that is shaping the way she lives her life. Fear of abandonment, shame and smothered rage are powerful limitations that no child would have to contend with if we, as adults, would make different choices. My parents were not to blame; they parented me to the best of their ability, probably similarly to how they themselves were parented. And so did I, thirty years later. But I certainly feel an urgency to recognize and reconsider the immense force that the mindless repetition of commonly accepted forms of censure and control in our family system is. Family systems have impact!

Claiming my rage each time as it surfaces, allowing it to move through my body and assimilate in my being, results in huge discoveries as new space opens up for joy and delight to flow into. I now have an awareness of what it feels like to flourish, and that feeling continues to deepen. I'm frequently inviting my sense of whimsy out to play. Imagine how different my children's and my grandchildren's lives would have been if I'd had the courage to unleash these aspects of myself earlier! I state this openly with regret and with honesty and clarity – and I know that by continuing to relax into myself more fully, I will enrich and enliven my life and the lives of others. It is a choice I am making mindfully.

I've written this chapter because I feel a tremendous urgency to share my experience of seeing though a different lens. As I continue to view my world from the WEL-Systems perspective, I have a renewed hope in myself, my family and even the planet. However, I am only a small thread in the universal tapestry and for change to happen at a scale large enough to really make a difference – for us, for our children's lives and our future - we need a major energetic shift of consciousness. It's clear to me now that to continue as we have been will not be enough. As Louise LeBrun's Foreword discusses, around the globe - which includes in our homes and schoolyards - we are currently witnessing serious challenges. Children inherit the results of the choices we make. As adults, as parents, as *guardians of a vision* for our children, we really can ask bigger questions and engage outrageous thoughts about who and what we are – and begin to really see what we are creating by not wavering from the 'tried and true' path we've been on.

As a woman, a parent and a grandparent, as the life force that I know I am in my physical body, I feel my powerful vibration pulling me forward. I am raising my voice against the pernicious, deafening and mind-numbing force of collective cultural conditioning; of generations of 'passing on the torch' of a family system within a paradigm that I feel is no longer adequate for the challenges we are facing now. I don't have answers but I know for certain that it's high time for each of us to have the courage to look at our families and our world through different lenses, to ask different questions and then, to engage mindfully.

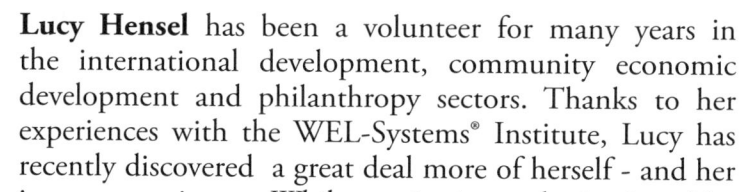

Lucy Hensel has been a volunteer for many years in the international development, community economic development and philanthropy sectors. Thanks to her experiences with the WEL-Systems® Institute, Lucy has recently discovered a great deal more of herself - and her journey continues. While continuing to be intrigued by photography, Lucy now claims her delight in painting and writing; these interests will be important for her as she moves into what seems like a new life, each day.

Combining her training as a CODE Model Coach™, her on-going discoveries about herself and how she sees her world, Lucy will be actively engaging with others and encouraging them to see life as the wonderful adventure it is.

RECLAIMING MY GODFORCE
Pat Donihee

If as a young woman I ever considered my future, I never considered anything other than 'married with children'. I do recall a few female students in my high school who were finishing Grade 13 and had plans to go on to unviersity but I cannot recall even one person in my Grade 12 graduating class with plans for other than nursing, secretarial school or teachers college - if they had plans at all. As I write that, a wave of heat moves through me and my forehead breaks out in a sweat. What small boxes we lived in and were expected to continue to live in! Now 50 years later, I am able to process the external control exerted on me to conform in all areas of my life; and the cost of my lifelong resistance to having someone else determine how my life was to unfold. Now I am able to reclaim what was lost to me: my birthright, my potential, my vision and my ability to shape the unfolding of my own life.

My call to contribute to this book has resonated deep inside my body, very much like the sound of a child's heartbeat on a sonogram - thump, thump, thump, thump - in resonance with my own heart. My own voice is in unison with the voices of others whose passion is a new paradigm - a paradigm that holds huge space in which to nurture the birthright, the potential, the vision and the genius of our children to shape their own constantly unfolding life moment to moment to moment.

It takes more than a village to raise a child. It takes the vision and the courage to name, on behalf of children, the patterns that break their will, crush their spirit, snuff out the flame of their potential and fill them with so much rage they are killing themselves and each other. Externally referenced, adult-centered authoritarian command-and-control parenting is destroying the future of our planet and our children.

Al Gore talks about 'an inconvenient truth' with regard to global warming and the world seems to pay attention. Who is speaking for children? Who is exposing the inconvenient truth about the current parenting programs? Who is acknowledging the birthright of our children? How is their uniqueness guarded, protected and provided with the conditions that make it possible for them to step into their potential as a birthright? It demands a new paradigm - a paradigm big enough to ensure respect, integrity and generosity of spirit moment to moment to moment…

My life-long relentless desire to be all I could be has kept me moving… moving towards I-knew-not-what for as long as I can remember. Each step in my evolution created a platform for the next unfolding, the next opportunity for me to be authentically present to me and, as a result, hold the capacity to be authentically present to others. I see what I see and hear what I hear with those in my world both on a personal level and on a professional level. Anything less than me moving through my world authentically would result in me shutting down when the conversation triggers a repsonse in my body and also shuts down the person with whom I am in conversation.

My uncompromising commitment to my own evolution led to me discover the WEL-Systems® body of knowledge. Living in a WEL-Systems paradigm taught me to soften my body so I can hear my messages from within and create space for the wave to move; and life changes for me. When my life changes, so do the lives of the children with whom I engage. My more stable vibration will align with the child or children I encounter and together we hold space for their spark to catch fire, to burn brightly until they are clear about how to hold their own vision for themselves in a much larger world of their creation.

I am a grandparent now because my children chose to have children and I am delighted about that! I must say I am also delighted that my active day-to-day, hands-on parenting days are behind me. A good thing, I'd say, as being fully and consciously present for a child, moment to moment, is the only thing that changes their world; and is the most vital activity in which we ever engage. Parents are the first and most important role models and teachers for their children, and if parents are lost in their own unmet childhood needs, it is virtually impossible for them to be present for their children. When we are not present to ourselves - authentically present to ourselves! - our children's potential is lost.

The fact that I am actively removed from the repetitive chores of caring for the children I interact with offers me a unique opportunity to notice parent-child interaction. The more authentically present I am to myself, the more aware I am of the impact of those interactions on children, especially noticing under what circumstances the child shuts down. Breathing is good! Teaching in the moment the way to belly breathe models moving inside and belly breathing opens space for the world to move.

I could weep when I think about how unconscious I was when my own children were babies and young children - and I would immediately if I thought it would make any difference! But I don't, simply because weeping can do nothing to 'undo' the way I was or anything I did. So I do what I can do: recommit myself to my own evolution and to decloaking. Decloaking is the one vital thing I know I can do that has the capacity to make a huge difference in my family. With respect, integrity and generosity of spirit (RIG[1]), I step into the moment and hear what my grandchildren are saying and not saying. I then open space for an authentic conversation with them and with their parents - conversations that I know are vital to the vision and potential my children hold for themselves in their own lives and in the lives of their children; conversations that have

---

1 *An Alternative to Love*, Louise LeBrun, *Spirit Crossing*, June 2009

the capacity to transform them and the way they relate to each other and to their children. I am completely unwilling to have these opportunities pass us by. I am unwilling to allow myself to ignore... to become unconscious to... what is happening and have another generation's internal flame collapse or be snuffed out by some physiologically altering material that numbs the God force we each are.

Command-and-control, adult-centered authoritarian behaviour dominated my life as a child and I know it dominated my parents' lives as well. *Authoritarian* parents are characterized as being highly controlling, requiring their children to meet an absolute set of standards. They are less flexible and lack responsiveness and warmth.[2] There were authority figures in each area of my life – family, extended family, church, school and even in my extracurricular activities like Brownies and Guides. It was all I knew and it was the way things were done then and I experienced the big stick of 'Do as I say or I'll hurt you.'

As a curious and questioning child, I quickly learned that if I kept up asking questions I would be 'brought into line.' I learned the line was whatever the particular authority figure wanted at the time. I learned the line moved. I learned without being aware of it, to be continuously looking for the line, to watch for any changes in the line, to feel safe. I learned to make myself small in an attempt to stay under the radar and I especially learned to doubt myself. After all, if I didn't give up my question or point, the intensity of the control went up; all the way up - at least in the all-girls Catholic school I attended - to the strap.

Sister Benedict kept a leather strap on her desk, used to exert her authority; and often, when we least expected it, slapping the desk to get our attention. It worked on me! I got strapped once for 'speaking out of turn' and never questioned her authority again... and for a long, long time I never

---

[2] Vulnerable Children, J. Douglas Willms, The University of Alberta Press, 2002, p.149

questioned anyone else's either, in any aspect of my life. Yes, the strap is gone from schools but how many other ways are used to continue to scare, to intimidate and to control a young child?

I didn't find respite from this command-and-control model anywhere in my life. I didn't even know enough to label it command-and-control until I was almost 50 years of age. My upbringing was after all, the era of 'children should be seen and not heard,' 'do as I say, not as I do' – an era from my day-to day experience, alive and well still.

My body held its first protest when I was eight or nine. I remember being doubled over with abdominal pain which had no basis in pathology, said the paediatrician my mother took me to. Then I began to bite my fingernails until they bled.

When I was almost 13, I developed eczema just on the palms of my hands; rendering me helpless to look after myself for even the basics of washing and dressing! The eczema manifested as big blisters full of liquid. Today I would say that my eczema was a brilliant response in my body and held pure genius! First, it got me a lot of attention and secondly, it got me admitted to hospital which made me someone to take care of rather than my usual role of taking care of others.

Taking care of others was a role created by a series of family circumstances and one I was rewarded for and learned very well. As a result of my hospitalization, I got to see firsthand whether all the Cherry Ames stories I had buried myself in for days on end were true! I got to follow the nurses around and see what they really did and I got to visit the younger children and play with them and keep them company, especially the younger ones who were so homesick.

I'm sure at 13 (I had my 13th birthday in the hospital) it all seemed like a great adventure. It also meant I had a summer off from helping out and baby-sitting at home with my younger siblings. I may have even thought the adventure was worth eczema! Who knows now? However what is fascinating to me in retrospect is that I had bouts of eczema all through high school and yet, once I moved two miles away from home and into residence to begin my three year hospital-based nursing program, I never lost a single day of training as a result of eczema!

Nursing school was another three years of a hierarchical, command-and-control environment where new students were clearly at the bottom of the pecking order ,subject to hazing by even the orderlies! We had curfews governing when we were able to leave residence, rules about how we lived in residence and especially rules governing our work on the floors at the hospital. Hotel Dieu Hospital was owned and operated by nursing Sisters who were very good at their jobs; and they certainly ruled the roost and everyone in it! Doctors were kings and everyone scattered when they arrived on the floor to review charts and write orders and only Sister talked to them – students were not even to be seen.

Despite the rules, I loved everything about nursing and I instinctively knew I was really good at it! Today I would say I was very good at building relationships, making a connection with my patients and in that environment, my patients knew they could get better and they did.

Three years of classes, studying, exams, hard work and camaraderie and suddenly, it was over. Each of us was to have an interview with the Director of Nursing before we were officially finished. When it was my turn, I approached her office with terror in my heart and fear about what she might say to me. I knocked, entered at her invitation and sat when she told me to. She sat behind her desk, resplendent in her white habit with only her eyes, nose, mouth and chin visible. "Miss Donihee," I recall her saying, "I consider myself a complete failure with you…." I know I gulped, probably held my breath and wondered what was coming next. Surely, not at this point could she do something to prevent me from achieving my dream! She continued, "...I have done everything I know how to do in the past three years to break your spirit and have failed completely." I don't remember much else about the interview except she gave me a holy picture with her name on it and dismissed me. I do know I had no idea about the real meaning of what she said to me – all I knew was I was done, free. My training was behind me, I was officially a graduate nurse and I had the signature on the form I needed to write my registration exams in September.

Many years later my insatiable curiosity and search for the answer would lead me to a book by Alice Miller, *For Your Own Good: Hidden cruelty in child-rearing and the roots of violence.* This book describes what Ms. Miller calls the 'poisonous pedagogy'. The following quote resonates with what was said to me in the interview with Sister Mantel so many years ago.

> It is quite natural for the child's' soul to want to have a will of its own, and things that are not done correctly in the first two years will be difficult to rectify thereafter. One of the advantages of these early years is that then force and compulsion can be used. Over the years, children forget everything that happened to them in early childhood. <u>If their wills can be broken at this time, they will never remember afterwards that they had a will, and for this very reason the severity that is required will not have any serious consequences.</u>

Though not a parent herself, Sister Mantle had learned well, in her own life perhaps, the lesson of break the spirit of the child so they become malleable to the will of the parent or substitute authority figure to respond without question to their command. She certainly failed with me and not for lack of trying!

If you think those days are behind us, think again. Command-and-control continues in every area of a child's life: parenting, families, in schools, in church, continuing to break the spirit of the child by whatever means... and at what cost? The cost is nothing less than the inherent birthright of every child; their right to their own potential; to the vision they carry for themselves to just be themselves, whatever that means.

Command-and-control, glossed over with whatever name you call it with the inherent destructive nature of "breaking a child's will", is killing not just the birthright of our precious children, its effects are killing our children as they use drugs, alcohol and sex more on themselves and each other to silence their inner message, and it must stop now!

For five decades, I lived in a world characterized by the inherent destructiveness of command-and-control as I moved through the stages of my life: school, nursing, training, marriage, children, separation and divorce. Just before my marriage ended, two things happened that would begin to offer me a glimpse of another way, new possibilities, a new paradigm. I got my first job outside of nursing and I started university.

University classes became the experience that turned my world upside down. It was like someone turned on a light switch after I'd bumped around in the dark for 40 years! Wow, way out there for me at that time, discussions outside the medical model, outside of the way I'd been conditioned and trained to think. That there was another lens through which to view the world was astounding to me and perhaps not just to me.

Other women friends, acquaintances were beginning to speak out, loudly and clearly, about things previously held to be 'private' like sexual abuse, violence against women and children. Yet for all our awareness we have made little progress, primarily because all efforts are taking place in an old, outdated allopathic medical model; a model based on Newtonian Science - the science of solving problems - rather than looking at a new paradigm altogether, the paradigm of Quantum Science. While millions of dollars are spent analysing the past, nothing changes in the every day life of children; and they are still being destroyed and destroying themselves in the place they most expect to be safe – their own homes! A child's home may be the most dangerous place they can be. Where on earth is the intelligence in that?

With new information, I did come to realize how unhealthy my marriage was and how I was done trying to fix what could only be what it was. Neither of us knew how to move beyond what we knew, what we had learned in our family of origin; and nor did we know where to look for something different. Neither of us knew how much we were hurting our children with our arguing and fighting, given the abuse in our relationship.

That we didn't know the impact on our children is no excuse and make no mistake: every child, every person who is unable to be exactly who they are every moment of every day is living in an abusive environment... an environment that sucks the life out of them and leaves no energy for them to develop their birthright, their potential and their vision for their own life. As parents, perhaps our greatest failure was that we never learned how to be present to ourselves. We never learned to step out of the parenting patterns that were passed to us from our parents and so we had no idea how to have our own healthy relationship.

Parting was the best choice we could have made for our children. It opened the door for us to begin to pay attention to our own evolution, not that I understood that word then! I did know that somewhere there was more, way more than I knew and much, much more that I didn't know. I wanted it for me and I wanted it for my children. I was like the ordinary seagull in the popular book *Jonathan Livingston Seagull*, I was never satisfied with who I was. I was always looking for the 'more' - whatever that was and trust me I didn't know what that was. I do know that today, as I have always known even when I couldn't name it, my ongoing evolution is my vital life force, as vital today as it always was when I was just a young child. Just imagine what my life might have been without years of chasing something out there, chasing what I knew I knew and couldn't name. Chasing what had been inside all that time! Imagine the world that will be created when every child is in an environment where space is held for them to be themselves always with no reservations to live the birthright of their own potential!

What I have learned is a powerful process for me to engage so that I have an edge to speak clearly and without any reservation about the inherent destructive force of unconscious, intergenerational authority-based parenting processes. That form of parenting is traumatizing our children. Trauma refers to "…the often debilitating symptoms many people suffer from in the aftermath of *perceived* life-threatening or overwhelming experiences.[3] " People, and especially children, who have been traumatized, can be overwhelmed by what we would consider normal, everyday events.

Trauma is about loss of connection - to ourselves, to our bodies, to our families, to others and to the world around us. This loss of connection is often hard to recognize, because it doesn't happen all at once. It can happen slowly, over time, and we adapt to these subtle changes sometimes without even noticing them. These are the hidden effects of trauma, the ones we keep to ourselves. We may simply sense that we do not feel quite right, without ever becoming fully aware of what is taking place; that is, the gradual undermining of our self-esteem, self-confidence, feelings of well-being, and connection to life.[4]

Trauma causes a disconnect from your sensory experience and the symptoms and patterns of behaviour are a result of this disconnection.[5] This disconnection deprives the

---

3 Levine, Peter A, PhD (2005) Healing Trauma. *A Pioneering Program For Restoring The Wisdom Of Your Body.* Sounds True: Boulder, CO. p.7.

4 Levine, Peter A, PhD (2005) *Healing Trauma. A Pioneering Program For Restoring The Wisdom Of Your Body.* Sounds True: Boulder, CO. p.7.

5 Levine, Peter A, PhD (2005) *Healing Trauma. A Pioneering Program For Restoring The Wisdom Of Your Body.* Sounds True: Boulder, CO. p.8.

individual of access to internal referencing (it deprives the person of the ability to access and respond effectively to cues from the environment - cues such as the distress a child may experience when yelled at, grabbed or handled roughly.)

Habituated parenting does not go quietly into the night. A traumatized parent, operating out of their intellect with no access to their own body messages, is incapable of being present for their child and so the pattern continues. It continues with children being brutalized emotionally, physically, spiritually or sexually; and when the system attempts to treat them mechanically, it is guaranteed the pattern will repeat itself and another generation of potential is wiped out. And yet, we wonder why our children take drugs, engage in dangerous sexual practices, cut themselves and take their own lives.

The system cannot be fixed! It requires a new paradigm and the new paradigm I have discovered is the WEL-Systems body of knowledge. In a WEL-Systems context, I have reclaimed and continue to reclaim moment to moment the God force I am... the God force I was created to be. I want that for every child.

M. Patricia Donihee, PhD, CCC, CODE Model Coach™ is a vibrant, energetic woman who moves through her world with intention and intensity. She is a woman committed to growing, learning and experiencing. This passion for life and her own inner flame of commitment to herself led her to the WEL-Systems body of knowledge.

As a Counsellor, Mediator, Coach and Custody Evaluator, Pat lives what she has learned and holds space for others to choose to step into their own deep end of the pool and their own potential. She is passionate about her commitment to represent the voice of children when they cannot speak for themselves.

A CALL TO GO BEYOND
Cathy Carmody

I was a parent once. I gave birth to two children, took on the identity of 'parent' and moved through the process of 'being' parent; all the while not really knowing whether I was doing things right or if I was a good and resourceful parent. For sure there were many times when I had no idea what I was doing, relying instead on memories of the ways in which I had been parented to take me through one crisis or another. I am currently the mother of two adult men and there are two things that I now know for sure:

- my role as parent, and my ability to hold any 'authority' over the lives of my two sons is long over and done with; and

- my ability to inspire and encourage an infinite number of others - including my sons and their families - to awaken to their limitless potential, will never be over and is in direct correlation to my willingness to become more.

I am now aware that whether I was a resourceful or un-resourceful 'parent' doesn't matter in the present or in the future. What does matter now, is that I am awake. Awake to the insights I've gained since my parenting days that the process of parenting, for me was the most important process that I could have engaged in throughout my lifetime, and is the one that is the most influential in the life of another human being.

Memories of Not Knowing

I wasn't totally aware at the time of 'being' parent that my influence on my children was as profound as it was. While I realized that my specific interventions with them about how to behave or think were having an influence in that moment, I was disconnected from the huge potential that my behaviors and who I was, would have on who they could become in the future. I moved through my role as parent without realizing that every aspect of my life reflected itself in my parenting. I had no semblance of knowing at the time, for example, that when I chose to silence myself in family conversations where I could have chosen to strongly put forth my views, I was a huge influence on my sons for their future interactions in conversations in similar situations.

I am now very aware that when I was in a parenting role, I was - for the most part - asleep! I parented my sons basically the same way that my parents parented me. I had no knowledge that I was in such a deep coma, nor did I realize that I was 'passing along' a lot of family history in the form of beliefs, attitudes, strategies and patterns.

I recognized that there was a lot about my early family system that was worth hanging on to. And, by the same token there was a lot that didn't serve me, including the rigid discipline of my father, the constant reminder of religion, and the way in which my mother never reclaimed or used her voice. These latter memories stayed buried in my body and moved along with me, flaring up from time to time, like a bush fire, as I grew older. I didn't realize the degree to which the fire in my body, held in the form of cellular memory, influenced my life and how easily and effortlessly I passed it along (unknowingly) to my children. Whether I liked the way I had been parented or not, when I was asleep - in my coma of habituated behaviors - everything from that early family system replicated itself in my life. All of it showed up, that which was good and that which was not so good; and, even downright painful.

The Coma of Habituated Responses and Behaviors

I've learned that none of us escape the coma of habituated responses and/or behaviors. It seems to be a massive reflection of our culture and the overarching control that exists, whether throughout the dogma around parenting, or throughout our religious, educational and political systems. It doesn't seem to matter - it is indeed everywhere. I've discovered that it is perpetuated and embedded in our culture and throughout the whole of our society.

Included in habituated behaviors is that of external referencing; of looking outside myself for validation of who I am, or what I do or say. Nowhere in my early family upbringing or my schooling was I ever taught to trust my inner knowing, my body, or my intuitive sense of what felt true for me. Always I was taught to defer to external authority figures whether it was my parents, teachers, work supervisors, various 'experts' or others. And to this day, it seems to me that everywhere I cast my eyes or tune my ears, I find myself being encouraged to look outside myself for advice on everything about me. It is as if we are highly addicted to looking for external validation. Seldom am I encouraged to take responsibility for my own health, my own sense of well-being, my personal power, my decisions about what 'feels' right for me, including decisions I need to make about my future work, my intimate life partner and ultimately, my life.

Waking up from the coma of habituated behaviors, including external referencing, and becoming 'conscious', happened for the most part after my children had grown up and left. However, something occurred during my parenting days that shifted the impact of my parenting. And while it had everything to do with me, it had a considerable impact on my sons. I consciously made a decision to change my life, and to move it forward. I chose to go back to university in order to improve my education and to ensure that I could provide in a more resourceful way for my sons. In the process of looking after, and putting myself first, I inspired my sons to become more.

I believe my sons learned by following in the path of my vibration, as well as through their own experiences. I like to believe that they continue to grow through my ongoing evolution, even though we no longer live together in the same house or even in the same city or province. In many cases their learning has been motivated by what they wanted to do differently because of my actions. And while they have their own challenges to face (as do the individual members of their families, including my three wonderful grandchildren), through it all, I am grateful for being able to bear witness to the ongoing evolution of each and every one of us.

I am often bemused by my seeming ability to move to a way of being where I have no 'holds' or 'restrictions' on who I can become as I age. As I move through my on-going years of 'being' grandmother, I believe my sons see, in my evolution, an invitation to step into the huge potential of their own ongoing evolution. This holds true as well for my grandkids who, at times, believe me to be pretty 'cool' because I am not the prototype of what has traditionally been known as 'grandmother' (or at least that's the story I make up about what they believe!).

Since my sons moved on to create their own lives, it has been a time of 'post-parenting' for me; a time during which I have experienced what I believe has been 'a call to go beyond'. To go beyond what I had experienced in my own process of parenting and to venture into a state of being that I never would have imagined myself entering. In this time I am choosing to respond to the call and create space to awaken others to their own journey of discovery.

I have met and worked with many women on my journey; mothers, and those about to become mothers, those who have never been or will be mothers - either by choice or circumstance - and the many who have lost sight of their birthright of potential as a result of how they have been parented. I have had the opportunity to invite many women to consider a different paradigm for their own self-awareness, for the growth of their consciousness and evolution, and for how they can choose to parent in a conscious way, rather than repeating the habitual patterns of the past.

Awakening

A specific event in my not too distant past was a call for a further, deeper awakening within me. I was working with a group of people in an organizational setting when I met a local aboriginal woman who had been invited to join us to share her experience of living forty plus years. In the stillness that followed her story, as the field around us vibrated with the memories of the inhumanities that our ancestors had imposed upon our aboriginal people, a thought – as crystal clear as ever one I can remember - came into my consciousness in the form of a question. "What is it that is happening right now, that years ahead in the future we will look back and wonder how we could have allowed this to happen?"

The answers came as quickly to me as the question: "It's the way in which children – our next generation – are falling through the cracks. It's the way in which I have known all along that the 'cracks' are there and yet have chosen, up until this point, to deny that I have any responsibility for the creation and maintenance of the cracks, or for the children and their mothers who were falling through them! It's the way in which I have allowed myself to move through my life in an unconscious, coma-like state, yet again. All the while assuming that the way things have been in the past are 'just the way they are' and will generally be in the future." I knew in that moment that it was about ME.

A sense of knowing swept through my body, like a wave crashing and washing up on a shore, speaking to me of the enormity of the challenge I had just unearthed, and in that moment, I knew I could not turn away. I knew that in whatever way I could, I would consciously reach out to make a difference. I didn't know how it would take form, just that it would. In that moment of reflecting on the children of others and in particular, the women who birthed and parented them, I could feel deep compassion and an equally deep need to work in ways that supported them in becoming more. In that moment of awakening, I knew, without having the words as I do now, that keeping myself in denial and silence for fear of evoking a confrontation, or challenging the status quo, or being humiliated or ridiculed, or for fear of hurting someone else's feelings was, and would continue to be, an excellent way to render myself powerless, diminished, small, and filled with fire and anger! All of which would eat away at the tissue of my body, causing my cells to go into a state of protection, and eventually, die; both metaphorically and literally.

I continue to know that staying silent about that which I know deep inside of me doesn't keep me safe, doesn't help me sleep at night, doesn't improve life for either myself or my family, my friends, my community or the world at large. Nor does it lengthen my life – and it certainly won't keep me from dying. I have become very aware that staying silent, and believing it to be a way of keeping myself safe, is a huge and powerful illusion!

And I know full well that there are no accidents in this life. During the period of time when I experienced that specific incident, I was also moving through what I can only call a huge acceleration and awakening of my whole being. I was immersing myself in a new body of knowledge (WEL-Systems®) and I was expanding and changing my model of the world, and the way I moved through it, at a rapid pace. Everything in my life became a metaphor for leaving my past behind. Old relationships both personal and business shifted and new opportunities sprang forth. It was as if the Universe was conspiring to move me into my work of the future. I remember traveling in Europe one summer during this time and coming home with a knowing that I did not want to see one more ancient church – ever, ever again! I had 'had it up to here' with history. I longed to totally explore new possibilities, without history as a reference point for my future.

Gradually I became aware that the way in which my work in the world would manifest in the years to come would take me and the women I attracted well ***beyond*** our comfort zones, well ***beyond*** what we already know, and well ***beyond*** our perceived notions, beliefs and ideas of what is possible for each of us. It would take us all into the field of our magnificent, untapped potential. At the time I didn't consciously know how this would influence each woman's ability to reconnect with herself as a parent, yet underneath it all it was there vibrating in a very powerful way.

Women and Me - Awakening continues

Over the past several years, as I have created the space for my work with women to evolve, I have witnessed how individuals go through incredible bursts of awakening - discovering through our work together, that they have been hiding for most of their lives, and have yet to find and reclaim their own, individual voices.

I have heard stories about the malevolent messages in the form of deeds, words, language and tone of the voice of authoritative 'others' that were communicated to young girls in their pre-teen and teen years in ways and with such intent, that they continue to vibrate in their bodies in their 30's and 40's and 50's. The impact of those early memories, buried in the cells of our bodies is enormous! For example, I will never forget the words of one woman who spoke out strongly about her reality, which is that at the age of 58, she still hears in her head, the voices of her mother and aunt telling her: "You will never amount to anything"!

All women can recall, seemingly word for word what was said to them, years ago. Voices pronouncing that they were too fat, too skinny, too slow, not smart enough, not pretty enough, not good enough, and on and on it goes. I am also aware that individuals seem to be largely unconscious (at least at the beginning of our work together) of the effect that their cellular memory has on their current behavior. They are, initially, unaware of how it stifles their potential, stifles their personal power; how it keeps them small, hidden away, silent for the most part, and unable to reclaim their innate brilliance.

Furthermore, they are totally unaware of how their unconsciousness keeps them locked into a model of 'parenting' their own children in total replication of the ways in which they had been parented. As we work together, peeling back layer upon layer upon layer of their cellular memory, I begin to hear new voices, authentic voices as they awaken from their deep sleep. I know that they are coming to realize that they are each the unique creator of their own lives. They are the creators of their own thoughts, intentions and beliefs. I am also witness to them, as they come to know – at a deep level in their body - that when the body is allowed to soften, open, process and metabolize old memories that no longer serve, we each become more.

Years ago, as a parent, it never entered my consciousness that my inner feelings were of any concern or of meaningful importance to my children. Based on what I knew and believed at the time, I saw my role as an external guide. I believed it was my job to create and set the rules, love them, encourage them and call them up if they broke the rules. I probably also used any number of empty threats, promises, and who knows what else, to ensure that they did as I wanted.

I do not remember ever stepping into sharing my deepest fears or other thoughts with my sons, not even when they became young adults. I never gave a moment's thought to opening up and exploring or explaining the reasoning behind my rules because in most instances, I didn't know or even pause to consider the reasoning, living as I was in my deep coma of habituated responses and behaviors. Nor did I believe at the time that they needed to know. I just didn't know what I didn't know.

In my process of working with women, I hear them express time after time, deep sadness about not knowing what their mothers/fathers were going through when the women were young children. I hear the stories of how their mothers/fathers would never, ever open up and share what fears they had - or continue to have - even today. I listen and bear witness when these very same women, as they listen to other women with similar stories, experience a softening and opening deep within them – and in that moment, they 'know' what they must do to parent and re-parent their own children differently.

My Willingness To Go Beyond

When I am willing to engage and be all that I can be and become in a program room full of women, I become more and so do they. When I am in the company of women who are yearning for something of which they know not, women who have a willingness to press forward, women who will challenge me and push me to discern whether or not I really mean what I say - then I know that I am in an energetic field that offers me the opportunity to go well 'beyond' the boundaries of who I have previously held myself to be, and into the realm of infinite possibilities.

I know that if in that moment I stray away from being totally and authentically who I am, I am letting them down. I am betraying them and I am betraying myself as well. By not staying with them in the moment and being true to myself, I miss the opportunity to become more. I miss the opportunity to show others that they too can become more by stepping boldly into their potential.

I also have learned through my experience in working with women that when I find the courage to share with my sons what is truly going on inside of me – about me - space opens for both them and me to become more. When I am willing to share with one of my sons that a long, lingering hug from him, a hug that deeply connects at an energetic level - me to him and him to me - means more to me then all the other external things going on, we both become more.

When I am willing to breathe, to allow energy to move and to metabolize, I am no longer a victim of my past – and my life expands exponentially. My future and that of each and every woman I touch, rests not in knowing 'how' to rid ourselves of the effect of our history, rather it rests in each of us being willing to soften and open our bodies, to breathe, to follow the impulses, and to allow ourselves to know our truths. The WEL-Systems® body of knowledge invites each of us to learn and integrate a ground shifting paradigm for stepping into this new way of being.

It always, always comes back to ME. In the same way that it always comes back to each of us, individually. The more I am willing to stand with an openness to that which I do not know; with a curiosity that is guided by an unlimited way of perceiving, with compassion and a reverence for other human beings, the more I create space to choose my inherent call to go beyond! In my circle of friends and those with whom I work, I experience a large number of individuals who see their lives almost entirely through the lens of their family, their friends and their immediate work – not necessarily in that order. Their propensity or willingness to go beyond that experience is often not present.

As I write these words, I know that it's all, and always, about me. I know that to write this statement honestly and authentically requires that I continue to look inward and ask myself : where in my life must I become more willing to stand strongly and courageously alone and speak out, even more

A Call to go Beyond

than I have previously done? How do I continue to increase my vibration in the world? How do I become the incredible change I want to see in the world and, in so doing, create the space for others to continually become more?

I am so grateful for the women with whom I work. There is not one who has not impressed me with their willingness to authentically show up in the room. Each moves in their own rhythm and in their own time. Each is unique. And as I work with these women, I see myself in each face. I see huge potential in each woman to change her individual life and the broader world around her Sometimes, I feel I can reach out and actually touch their potential. It feels so concrete and yet, I know it is much more than that which I can see and touch. It is an energetic field so potent and so powerful that as we engage, I feel my own potential unfolding.

While I could sit and pass recriminations against those parents whose un-resourcefulness has left countless women and men wandering through the future of their potential without guide posts, it seems to me that if each of us as human beings – whether we have given birth or fathered a child of our own or not - focused on opening up to our own unique potential; if we chose to act in our own way to make a difference in the world, our inspiration for those wandering in the wilderness of their potential might light a spark which could grow into a very bright light.

I believe that my 'call to go beyond' is not about having the answers nor is it about knowing what's right or wrong for each or any one individual. It is about creating space for myself and every individual I come in contact with, so that we come to know the power that each of us holds within our body. It is the power to stay in the 'questions' that move each of us forward on our individual journeys of ongoing discovery - discovery of our own limitless potential.

My call provides an incredible opportunity for me to go beyond 'being parent', long after my traditionally defined 'parenting' role has left the room. By choosing to remain open to hear my call and then acting on it, I have become an infinite and ever increasing vibration that echoes well beyond my parenting. For me, that has been - and will continue to be - a powerful and wonderful thing!

Cathy Carmody is a woman who has walked many paths, always pressing the edges of possibilities and growing younger by the day. She believes her life to be an on-going adventure, continually unfolding as a reflection of her beliefs. Cathy lives her life's passion by creating and offering programs and services that inspire and guide women – and courageous men - on their path toward the full expression of their potential. Keeping her company on her journey is an equally evolving life partner who is discovering an unfolding passion in the mid-stage of his life.

IT TAKES A COMMUNITY
Debbie Elliott

I grew up in simpler times, and I truly lived the adage that it takes a community to raise a child. Adults were all treated equally and a parent was a parent, whether mine or not. I learned that they were always right, always had the answers. I also grew up with the saying, "children should be seen and not heard" and "do as I say, not as I do", the latter one being a little hard for me. I was naturally curious, yet felt that I could not ask questions about the conversations that were floating around in my head. It left a lot to my imagination! Words got twisted and images were extraordinary, to say the least; and believe me, a lot of confusion could have been cleared up if I had only been encouraged to ask questions.

I remember when I came in contact with death for the first time. A young man in our community had a pilot's license and was due in town that afternoon. It was a Friday. All of us kids kept looking up to the sky. We wanted to be the first one to see the plane, but it never came. I remember the whispered conversations of the adults as they spoke about how it was too late and dark to be flying into the mountains, and he probably decided to wait until the next day. I can still feel that sick churning in the pit of my stomach as the doorbell rang the next morning and I was given the key to the town library. They wanted me to open up. Since I spent a lot of time there, this was not too unusual, but that feeling that there was something horribly wrong would not go away.

As the day grew longer, the feeling was more intense. No one came to the library to relieve me, which was not normal. I returned home to find my Mom ironing with tears streaming down her face, as my father burned his clothes in the fireplace. I was never told what it was all about. As children, we pieced it together: how the plane had crashed in the mountains, how my father had been the one to spot them from the search helicopters, how he was covered in blood and tried to do something but they were already dead. I remember lying on my bed crying in anguish, afraid and wanting so badly to understand; to tell my father how proud I was that he tried; to have someone explain how this could happen.

Instead, we were sent outside to play as all the parents congregated in living rooms, never realizing the grief and anxiety that we were experiencing. Today, we have grief counselors but I am not sure they can take the place of an honest, free-flow of conversation and emotion between parent and child. What I needed was to be held; to be told the truth, no matter how much it hurt. If those conversations had taken place, my fears may not have manifested into the fears of an adult. Unspoken conversations tended, for me, to become the seeds for fears that grew and grew unless I kept them locked away. I spent a lifetime hiding my true feelings. It was what I learned to do and it no longer is how I live my life, thanks to the discoveries I have made through WEL-Systems®.

I spent my childhood pushing boundaries. I became very good at strategizing and often would weigh my options, knowing full well the consequences of my actions, and then do it anyway. I was the one to do something just because I could, just because I was told not to and, my favorite, just to see what it felt like. I was always aware that the punishment, should I be caught, would include being grounded, or confined to my bedroom or the yard (during the summer months). With this in mind, I usually had a contingency plan. I would go to the local library and take out about a dozen books which I then proceeded to hide under my bed, for the eventuality that this would be where I would serve my sentence.

I became euphoric about conquering my demons, whatever they were that particular week. I did everything from skiing down blind alleys, to jumping off the highest diving board. I remember riding inner tubes on the river, being pulled along by the current on hot summer days (something we girls would have been skinned alive for had our parents found out), and I remember the feeling of power when we did it. I remember conquering my fear of walking across the top handrail of the foot-bridge, never really being aware of what would happen if I fell. I remember racing my bike straight down the biggest hill with my feet up on the handlebars - and being caught. That time, the punishment was taking my bike away for the rest of the week.

It was by pushing the boundaries that I released what raged inside of me: my need for attention that today, would probably be diagnosed as Opposition Defiant Disorder (ODD). When the messages from my body became too strong for me to ignore any longer, I screamed for attention. Any attention! My mother did not know what to do with me when I would act out, and it was during those times that the phrase "she's your daughter, you talk to her" rang throughout our home. My father would shake his head in despair and ask me why, and with the wisdom of a child I would respond: "Because!"

'Because' was the word that explained what drove me to explore the universe outside those boundaries that had been set. I could not find the words for the feelings that were raging deep inside of me. Like many of my generation, my parents were so busy trying to provide for us that emotional needs were not taken into consideration and maybe, just maybe, they didn't know how to address my inner needs. Tears and fears were brushed aside or made light of. As a child, I soon recognized that certain conversations made adults uncomfortable, so I decided never to talk about emotions or feelings again; to just do whatever I needed to do to avoid expressing myself so no one would see that side of me again.

For example, I had heard all my young life that there was something wrong with my mother; that she was depressed, which translated to 'she was crazy', in my mind as a child. I listened to grown-up conversations and I couldn't understand what they meant. I was so sure that there was something wrong with me. "Who knows?", I thought, "Maybe I am crazy, too".

I decided at the age of ten not to have children. I was so afraid that I would do the same thing to my child, that I felt had been done to me. I was afraid that I would somehow neglect to nurture their soul while focusing on providing the material aspects for their lives. And while I would instill the ethics that would make them a good person in the eyes of the world, somehow or other, I would neglect to encourage them to dream, to create, to imagine; would neglect to inspire them to be all that they could be. I imagined that I would be so afraid that I would feel resentful of the time it took to do the job properly. What if I was crazy? Did that mean I would have crazy children? That was not going to happen - it stopped there and then.

When I met my soul mate and decided that I did want to have children after all - that between us we could raise a child - circumstances were such that I could not conceive. I spent many years filled with guilt, believing that maybe I was being punished for my rash thinking when I was a ten-year-old child.

Not having children left me like the proverbial child at the candy store... face pressed against the glass, toes scuffing the pavement... as people passed me by, stopping to have those meaningful discussions only with others of the same culture, the same conditioning - others who were 'parents'. I felt like one of those bobble-heads that you put on the dash of a car: I could listen and nod but not dare to offer an opinion.

I could not have children. That did not render me stupid, yet people just assumed that I did not understand; or they took great lengths in explaining things to me. I have been told that I have absolutely no idea about how hard it is to raise a child, in this day and age; that I do not know anything, for how could

I, I have never given birth. I have been told to "get with the program"; "that's just the way things are these days"; "you'll never know so how dare you have an opinion". At one point, I had a lady explain to her 5 and 7 year-olds - in great detail and in her mother tongue - that I cannot have children, while I helplessly stood by. A lifetime of insecurities flooded me; all those feelings of not fitting in, not belonging. I remember thinking "God, I can't even get this right".

So I began wondering, why was I here? What was my purpose? It was obvious that I missed the boat on 'go forth and procreate', so what was I to do? I felt ashamed, frustrated, terrified and alone, all at once. I would never get to cuddle my own child, wipe their tears or kiss their cuts and scrapes; and I would never, never fit in, no matter how hard I tried, no matter how much I wanted to. As my friends and family had children and moved forward with their lives, I would be left behind in the dust, to wander on my own. The word 'family' did not and would not apply for me, at least, not in the traditional sense.

I started slowly to pull back from everyone... from life. I went back to my saving grace as a child and buried myself in books and creative endeavors. I tried my hand at everything from knitting to macramé, from sewing to cross-stitching. Nothing filled the void for very long. I went from project to project, craft to craft, book upon book. My restlessness was explained away as wanting to learn, being homesick or just a sign of the seasons. Not once did it occur to anyone - even me! - that I was trying to occupy my mind so as not to feel the pain inside of me. As I denied my pain, locking it down, it was as though my light was slowly being smothered. I believed that the joys and sorrows I witnessed my friends experience from the sidelines was not ever going to be present in my life. There were friends and family who tried to include us but after a while, the pain of being told constantly and consistently to look but not touch, also took a toll on my life. Withdrawal was the easiest way to stop the bleeding.

I admit it: I wanted to be just like all those women we saw in the magazines; the ones that were perfect with perfect hair, body, job and family. Every May as Mother's Day approached, I would be assaulted by the commercialization of the perfect family: mother and child/children - family in its highest form. I felt constantly reminded how I did not fit in, how the family unit should resemble that of the Cleavers.

The cycle would repeat itself as Father's Day rolled around, bringing up all my feelings of guilt. The guilt used to consume me and I would do anything to escape. Yet, not once was it because of anything my husband said. It was instead, a direct result of my old memories of not measuring up. I would wallow deep within myself, feeling as though the whole world knew we did not exist as a family unit. Because I blamed myself, I imagined that everybody blamed me, too. Now, I know deep in my body that the image of the perfect family is a myth created by advertisers. Perfect families, like perfect bodies, just do not exist.

When I was a child, I remember running hard and long until I collapsed on the ground, tears streaming down my face and my heart racing; the scent of the grass filling my nostrils; the warmth of the sun on my back as I lay sobbing with my young heart about to break. All this because my brother had said something or other that, at the time, completely devastated me. As my heart stilled and the tears stopped, I got up, brushed myself off and went on with my day. I would quickly forget what was said but it was that feeling of relief - the calm after the storm so-to-speak, that I remember to this day; the release of that pent-up energy - was what I needed to go on; what I needed for me to move forward.

It is *that* peace - that calmness and clarity - that I was seeking in my adult life, when I withdrew into the imaginary world of books or the preoccupation with crafts and hobbies to dull my pain. It is *that* spent emotion - that movement of energy in my body; the release of what was locked down inside me that I had desperately needed to control to survive as a child - and *that* relief that I felt I could no longer access as I grew older.

By the time I was an adult, I was conditioned to believe that in order to be a good girl/woman, I was expected to 'suck it up'. I learned to lock down my body to try to manage the sensations that were moving inside me. Since discovering a new perspective through WEL-Systems, I know that my body can guide me; that those sensations are energy and information and are not 'good' or 'bad' - they are simply reminders of information waiting to be integrated into the whole of my being. I now trust and relax into the sensations that used to send me off into my old escapes of crafts and reading. By embracing this wave in my body, I no longer feel like a victim of my circumstance. I can claim these experiences with ease by simply breathing and relaxing my body. I now move forward in my life with the same sense of calm and clarity that I knew instinctively how to create when I was a child.

I grew up believing that my parents had all the answers and that they were somehow born our parents. Then, as I grew older, I was taught that teachers and professors, aunts and uncles, and the whole adult world knew everything and had the answers to all that exists in the universe. I have to wonder what it would have been like if the adults in my life had encouraged me to trust the energy and information moving in my body rather than teaching me how to control and manage it.

I wonder how differently my life would have unfolded if, rather than ignoring me because they were uncomfortable with what it called up in them, the adults in my life would have been willing to have open, honest conversations. As a child, I may have surprised them with the honesty of my answers and the courage of my questions. If I had felt safe to talk about the fears that were burning like wildfires within me, would my life have been different? If I had asked about my mother's absences, instead of listening to the gossip of adults and filling in the blanks with the overactive imagination of a child, would I have felt safer?

Through the lens of my experiences, I have watched children grow up without imagination, inspiration and open communication; their creativity dulled or lost from the constant control and conditioning as to when or how to use it. I have watched while the dreams that fill them became mingled with the dreams that others instilled in them, until they aren't really sure where their dreams end and someone else's begins. I have observed how expectations flow from one generation to the next with little or no thought for the individual. I have witnessed children growing into adults who are afraid to disappoint and are therefore afraid to try; never quite reaching outside their comfort zone, buffering their success by making it dependent on their ability to shift and change to meet the expectations of those around them.

In my experience, children are taught to be mindful of others and to put everyone and everything else above their own needs. They are taught how to lock down their bodies, just as I was, rather than how to trust the intelligence that it carries. Knowing what I know about my own experience, I can't help but feel terrified at the challenges that today's children face as old patterns continue to repeat, generation after generation.

Today, as I face my fiftieth birthday, I realize that I have finally relaxed into the sensations and experiences held deep within my body for all those years. I can now put words to all the emotions surrounding my not having given birth. Tears fill my eyes and I relax into them with ease. As the sun streams in my window, and with my dogs curled up by my side, the tears subside for I have finally told my story. I feel a deep contentment after releasing what I have held inside for so long. I realize that this is part of what makes me who I am.

I also have come to realize that I am more than 'the woman without a child'. I no longer see myself as a misfit - I am moving ahead with life! I have a lot to offer and now, instead of wallowing in self pity; instead of denying how I felt, I face each day with childlike wonder, for I know it will be as great as I allow.

I still love to push boundaries, explore possibilities and to create. I know that I will continue with this new way of living, trusting myself and the messages from inside, instead of believing that others know what is best for me. I have learned that if I allow my body to guide me, if I ask the questions, if I have the courage to be, then I am right where I need to be. I will create the life that I want, and I will do it with confidence and love. I know that by finally acknowledging how I feel and how I felt, trusting my body to metabolize with ease and speed the energy and information that was locked down, I have started to learn to love and believe in myself, again.

Parenting does not come with a handbook, although many have been written that were based on an old paradigm. We are still teaching children to do the very things I have spent the last number of years learning to undo. Wouldn't it be an amazing world if children were taught to be open and honest; were taught to *trust* that energy and information that moves within each of us; were taught that without blame or judgment, they can move through their lives to the beat of their own drum by following those internal cues; and that in doing so, will become the magnificent human being that they were born to be. At fifty, this is what I have rediscovered and it required a new paradigm, one that is available through a WEL-Systems perspective. "It takes a community to raise a child" - and I am an important part of that community.

> Since being introduced to the WEL-Systems® body of knowledge in 2007, **Debbie Elliott** has never looked back. Fully conscious, she now moves forward on her accelerated journey, encompassing all there is, constantly growing, and sharing her story with those around her.
>
> Debbie carries a deep intention to live her life in the moment. She continually evolves her writing; and invites and supports all those with whom she works and plays to become aware of what is possible for them if they, too, are willing and open to explore that which they don't know that they don't know.

IT'S NEVER TOO LATE

Noreen Mejias

When I was invited to contribute to this body of work, at first I was taken aback and thought to mySelf, "Why me? I have never been pregnant. I have never given physical birth to another human being. What would I have to write about and contribute, anyway?" All notions based upon my perceived view of parenting. Did I really have anything to write and to say on the topic? I toyed with the idea and eventually dismissed it.

Some weeks later, I read the Foreword that Louise LeBrun had written. After reading just the second paragraph, 'something' awakened in me and beckoned, propelling me forward. The pull was so strong that I was lost in my world of reflection for over an hour; all this after just reading those two paragraphs. The words: **boundless potential** that we all are; parenting as a context for **accelerated evolution**; parenting as a **safe space** within which the biological imperative of growth can easily unfold and express in ourselves; parenting to become **guardians and facilitators and invitations to greatness**; parenting to become the **seed of potential, that sources tomorrow** spoke to something deep inside me.

The 'something' that awakened was ME! Glorious, brilliant and imperfect Me. Me awakening again and lusting to engage again in my own Life! I literally shook and shuddered as waves of emotion and energy washed over me. The palms of my hands and my underarms started to perspire: I felt drenched. I was so moved that I wept. As the tears rolled down my cheeks, I remembered to inhale and to exhale and to take great big gulps of air. I remembered to lift my head up and to remove my hands that were covering my eyes. I remembered to keep my eyes wide open as the waves of energy washed over me again and again. And in the aftermath and stabilization of my body came the quiet calm. And then the welcomed insights and wisdom came flooding into my sense of awareness.

I remembered my own biological imperative to grow. I remembered my need to expand, my need to create and my need to explore. I remembered my hunger to live and to be fully alive. I remembered my passion to be unleashed and to reclaim and to fervently embrace the limitless possibilities of my own birthright.

Now, on reflection, my old limiting belief of only giving birth as a definition of what it was to be a parent flew out the window and dissipated. I realized that ownership and bloodlines had nothing to do with parenting and guardianship. I knew, beyond a shadow of a doubt, that I, too, had something I wanted to say and to acknowledge and to honor: first to mySelf and then out loud to the wider audience of the Reader.

I feel very passionately that I am one of the "Guardians of the Vision" and my mission, on this watch, is to eke out and to awaken the potential in mySelf and in others, no matter what the age! That, for me, is my contribution to PARENTING; and in so doing, I feel that I have made a conscious, mindful contribution. I have engaged in Life and allowed my world and theirs to expand majestically.

As a Chartered Professional *Strategic Wealth* Advisor (Ch.P.), I have come to experience clients from all walks of life. I have had the privilege of my clients entrusting their financial / investable assets to me, as steward and guardian of their vision. In many ways, I have also become the Guardian of their potential; the potential often left untapped, having been shelved while they committed themselves to the obligations and responsibilities that made up their early years. For many, they have never had the opportunity to engage with someone who is willing to be present to them and with them, as they seek to awaken to the majesty of who they are capable of becoming - regardless of age!

The supposed intention is to make the investable asset grow so that they may be able to use this resource to experience the life of their choosing. The notion that they, too, will be able to fulfill the life of their dreams; they, too, will be able to claim the birthright of their own potential! And yet, so often this is not the case. I have found that the money - the investable asset - does not bring the quality of life my clients are seeking. At times, I feel this fixation on amassing money actually prevents people from accessing their full potential.

I see more often than not, no purpose, no vision fulfilled. The money that was being scrimped and saved, now that it is amassed at the point called retirement, doesn't seem to bring the vision or the purpose to fruition. In some instances, I see money still being saved even though the amounts are in the millions. So often I hear the sentiment that "It can't just be spent and wasted on me!" Questions arise such as: "Am I really deserving of all this money? What are my choices, anyway? Who am I becoming? I'm getting older and I have no real sense of who I am."

I hear the angst and wrestling with oneself; and the final acknowledgement and awakening that it is not about the money, after all. As we finally come to the realization that we can only distract ourselves with so much golf; so many world cruises; so many shopping expeditions; so much food; so much alcohol; so much plastic surgery, and so much volunteer work. It is a scary place, it seems, when we have to wake up to our lives that have become routine and habituated. We seem to have forgotten the birthright of our own boundless potential in ourselves, far less in trying to evoke this birthright of boundless potential in those we love and care about.

I know only too well about the rage, the feelings of betrayal, the worry, the loss of control, the sleeplessness, the loss of identity, and the loss of the sense of self around money that accompanies the fear: Will I lose it all?"

What follows are a few reflections of my journeys of my own Self-discoveries. I have found that in sharing the stories of the journey of my Life with others, without giving any answers, I have become the invitation for my clients and those that I come into contact with, to awaken to the brilliant geniuses that they are. In turn, we discover (and we are in the continuous process of discovering and uncovering) the abundance, and sheer joy and delight that life has to offer. We can mindfully shape and design lives of our own, choosing new and different opportunities. We remember that we are not small and puny and helpless, rather we can evolve and live by our own unique intentions.

I know, beyond a shadow of a doubt, that we are all very powerful human beings when we look inside ourselves, without having to resort to outside (externally referenced) distractions. Distractions that may come in the form of medication and other drugs to find the 'quick fix' so that we can return to the illusive state of 'normal'. Distractions of excessive alcohol, or excessive overeating, or going to the latest therapist (sometimes for years on end). Distractions of our cultural conditioning which leaves us worrying about what others might think of us. All of these distractions are strategies to help us try to forget and numb the pain and to diminish the movement and flow of energy in our bodies, all in the misguided notion that something is WRONG with us . . . we don't fit in; we don't belong; we don't conform to the collective. The so-called 'pain' or 'dis-ease' in our bodies is an invitation to force us to sit up and to *mindfully* pay attention to the lives that we are living and creating for ourselves; lives which at times, just aren't working because they are not a reflection of who **we *really*** are.

We are all very powerful, UNIQUE human beings when we are internally referenced. Powerful human beings with resolve and great capacity to create rich and expansive and meaningful lives for ourselves, by our own design and intention; lives worthy of living. Lives in which we guard and cherish our vision. It is our vision that pulls us into growth and discoveries about our potential and ourselves. It is our vision that gives us choice and direction and our ability to create and to explore and to get curious about different opportunities. Our VISION propels us into being all that we possibly can be: with unlimited possibilities, with unlimited POTENTIAL.

One of my roles as a Life-transition Advisor is to help my clients to plan financially for the expected and the unexpected life transitions that may occur in the future. We help clients to enjoy life, planning for the future, creating financial comfort, minimizing taxes, examining estate planning choices, charitable giving, legacy building options, long term care options, as well as end of life issues. What role will their finances play? What is their VISION?

But if that were all that I did within the bounds of my theoretical, analytical training, I would remain trapped and leashed and locked into my intellect. What lights me up and gives me meaning, is engaging authentically with my clients. Having meaningful conversations with them, that are intimate and personal about the things that really matter: things that hold deep significance and meaning for them. And as I have found over the years, the 'it' in the question "what is it that's truly important to you?" is NEVER about the currency we label as MONEY!

So often I see lives that are wasting away as the essence of being mindlessly drains away. I see lives with lots of wealth that are lived without access to potential – joyless lives, passionless lives, insipid lives, lives full of mediocrity; lives that are habituated and mindlessly lived in a coma with no connection to Self. I have witnessed lives where growth has been stunted and denied.

In other cases, I see lives where the fragile seed of potential, the seed of accelerated evolution of becoming MORE, is left to wither and shrivel away. I know there are people who are literally dying, riddled with dis-ease and dis-content! At times I want to say, "Wake-up to yourself! You do have choice! You do have alternatives! Grab a hold of your Birthright! Wake up to your own Potential! Your Potential is waiting in the wings, pleading to be unleashed! Your potential yearns to be set free, in order that you may soar again in all your own magnificence and glory. Your potential beckons, and wants to propel you into becoming the Genius you are meant to be. And, you are never alone!"

As an example, I saw a young man recently who had obtained my name and particulars from the Internet. He was an engineer, had his Ph.D. in Engineering and was very techno-savvy. He told me he had done his research and analysis of the financial business well. He said he was calling to make an appointment to see me; and made it quite clear that he was interviewing and had interviewed a number of potential candidates to be his advisor.

He arrived with his laptop computer in tow, set it on the table and opened it up to his list of questions. He had lost a great deal of money trying to manage his money on his own. He felt that he now needed assistance and wanted to ensure that he was making the right decisions by picking the most appropriate Financial Advisor. What did I think of his pick of A, B, and C stocks? What did I think of gold as a pick for his portfolio? What did I think the dollar was going to do? What did I think of the current market volatility? What were the fees? What was my process?

Absolutely nothing fired in me as I sat and listened to the barrage of questions. I responded to many of his questions by saying "I haven't got a clue". He seemed taken aback and proceeded to close his laptop. Others had had analytical opinions and answers to his questions. I merely shrugged my shoulders and smiled.

And yet something moved in me such that I wanted to engage in a meaningful conversation with this restless, agitated young man. I was just not willing to send him on his way. I proceeded to have a chat with him about where he was going in his Life and about the Quality of his Life. What was important about money, to him? What was important about being Alive, to him? What is it that lights him up? What was his vision of what he wanted in life; his hopes; his dreams? Who was he becoming? He sat transfixed and speechless. For a moment, I thought he was getting ready to grab his computer and run screaming from the room.

Then, he slowly began to speak and to engage with me, genuinely and authentically. I wasn't surprised when the young man very politely asked whether I would consider taking him on as a client. For my part, I accepted the invitation for here was someone willing to engage in a meaningful conversation. Here was someone who was mindfully choosing to stay awake, and to step into his own potential. For me, here was an opportunity to engage also and be a "Guardian of Potential".

At the other end of the spectrum, my 94-year old client has awakened to her own potential, through our continued meaningful conversations. Life has become fun and playful once more, filled with a sense of curiosity and excitement along with a sense of adventure. After the death of her husband and partner of many years, she began to lose hope and felt disconnected from being truly ALIVE. Her health started to deteriorate. Family members were no longer close by, as many had died or lived far away and in some cases, out-of-province. She and her husband never had any children and had scrimped and saved and sacrificed all their lives in order to attain the assets they had acquired. She had the millions, but now what? There had to be more to Life than this, wasn't there? How could she partake in a meaningful life and stay connected to her Self? Could she make a contribution to humanity that had nothing to do with money? What were her limiting beliefs around scarcity and danger that were holding her back? What were the belief systems that were no longer serving her? She wanted her

Life to matter. We discussed and played with these questions, not seeking answers. I was amazed that my client was simply willing to "be". She is very much awake and she was willing to allow the meaningful conversations to rumble around inside her body. Many a time shaking her head and saying to me, "I don't know about that one".

My client has awakened at the age of 94 and reclaimed her own potential to live a meaningful life and in turn, is able to become the guardian of potential for her family. She takes great delight in assisting her nieces and grand nieces, and not only financially. She is a sounding board to them as they, too, bump against the challenges in their lives. She wants to have her own meaningful conversations with them.

At her last medical check-up, she told me the doctors said that her health has improved tremendously and that she is in remarkable physical condition. She looks at least 20 years younger than her current age. She told me recently that she intends to live until at least 107 and I've no doubt that she will!

On a very personal note, I remember the notion of parenting to my parents. I recall how I parented my mother in particular, during the last few years of her life. My parents lived in Trinidad and after the death of my father from Alzheimer's, my mother's health deteriorated rapidly. She was eventually diagnosed with Parkinson's disease. She did not have the constant tremors and shakes that normally come with the disease, instead she was very unbalanced in her movements and was unable to get around without the assistance of her two walking canes, or her walker. On the referral of a friend, my brother and I hired someone to stay in the house with her. Being so far away in Canada, I did not personally interview the live-in helper and relied on my mother's judgment. Things seemed fine, and although it was not the ideal situation, Mum said she was making the best of it.

Suffice it to say, that things with the helper went from bad to worse. Eventually it was revealed that this person had a terrible temper and was not only mentally terrorizing my mother, but from the number of falls and bruises my mother endured, I am convinced that my mother was physically abused as well. My mother was inclined to explain it all away by saying that the helper, who was 62, had had a difficult life. When the so-called 'flare ups' would occur, the person was always very sorry and contrite, and would not only ask for forgiveness, but she'd go to Church to confess the evil wrongs she had committed. "After all," Mum said, "no one was perfect", patience and tolerance were required, and trying to get live-in help with someone you could trust was very difficult to find.

My brother and I didn't buy any of that rubbish and hurriedly flew down to Trinidad. We gave the woman notice that she was to leave immediately; and if she was still there when we arrived at the house, she would be physically removed and her belongings dumped out on the street.

I remembered lying in the bed with my mother, after the episode had played itself out and the distasteful person was gone. We talked and chatted and reminisced about the old days with fond memories. My mother was 88 years old. Her body had further deteriorated with the advanced Parkinson's disease and she had difficulty getting herself out of bed. We had to face the discussion of what was going to happen going forward. Who was going to look after mother, once my brother and I left Trinidad to return to our lives in Canada?

In bed talking to my mother that night, I said to her "Mum, you know in this life you still have choices, even though your body seems to have betrayed you and you seem stuck and unable to move and get around. You are not really stuck; you still have, and will always have the dignity of choice. You still have control and a right (a birthright) to say yes or to say no! No explanation, no reasoning, no having to rationalize your decision to anyone. Just the right to say yes or to say no: just because it feels right to you and because you say so. We are past the stage of you trying to continually help others, at the sacrifice of your own dignity and self worth. It is time that you were Self-ish and put yourself first because YOU are important! You are not small, puny and insignificant. YOU are important, and your life really matters!"

"Mum, what if we ran an ad in the newspaper and advertised for the ideal type of person that you wanted to look after you. What if you had the opportunity to interview the candidates, and you got to choose the person who felt just right for you: not right for anyone else, but just right for you."

My Mum started to cry. I remember taking her in my arms and holding and hugging her to myself: her small, very frail, bone-like body. "I love you Mamma", I said. "I won't let anyone hurt or harm you ever again."

"I love you too dear", she said. As the trembling and stutters and pulses of energy and information moved and shuddered in her thin, waif-like body, all I could remember to tell her was to breathe.

"Breathe Mamma, breathe." And I showed her how to breathe, by breathing deeply myself: great, big gulps of air, as the tears also rolled down my face. As the body tremors of energy and information-in-flow slowly subsided, a quiet calm seemed to follow. We eventually fell asleep in each other's arms.

The next morning I woke up in bed alone! "My God", I thought, "where was my mother?" She had been asleep beside me hours before. This was a woman who for the last two years could not get out of bed unaided. She couldn't possibly have gotten out of bed by herself, far less without me waking up and hearing her. I called out and couldn't seem to find her anywhere in the house. She couldn't simply have vanished. Her walker was still in the bedroom, so it was impossible for her to be outside! Panic started to set in, and I called out again frantically.

"I'm here dear", came my Mother's clear voice, from outside. I went to the back door and stood transfixed and speechless. I couldn't believe what I saw before my eyes.

"My God Mum, what are you doing?" I said flabbergasted.

"I decided to sweep up the leaves in the yard", was my mother's cool response. Broom in hand, she smiled, as if this were an everyday occurrence. "Something has changed," she said. "I woke up with my body feeling so good, that I decided to come outside for some sun and fresh air and noticed all the leaves strewn about, so I decided to tidy up a bit. It's good exercise you know".

Flabbergasted doesn't begin to describe what I felt. The physical change that I witnessed in my Mother was indescribable. She didn't seem to want to make a fuss or to acknowledge what had transpired. She didn't want to analyze or to dissect her feelings. She didn't want to find answers to what had occurred as to her newly found ease of mobility. For her, it was as simple and easy as "a breath", the night before.

True to our word, we ran an advertisement in the newspaper and interviewed about 20 applicants. Mum got to ask the questions, her voice clear and strong. It was magnificent to witness my mother once again in all her glory. She was "unleashed" and pulled herself up to her full Potential. In fact, she seemed to have grown in height and stature. When Mum's special gerontology doctor came by the house for a visit, she too was dumbfounded. Change wasn't supposed to be instantaneous. Maybe this was an unusual form of the disease, she had pondered.

The above took place in March 2005. Two months later on June 7th, 2005 my mother died. While going to the bathroom (unaided) in the early morning hours, she stumbled and fell, striking her head on a hard surface. I was devastated. I wish I had been there to somehow prevent it. I had hoped that by hiring all the various attendants to look after Mum, with apparent round-the-clock care, this would have somehow prevented her from dying. Silly perhaps, in wanting to wrap up those we love and guard them against any misfortunes, as I guess any "parent" would.

Still I feel honored and proud to have had the privilege of being a witness to my mother's remarkable transformation that day in March. I had been able to create a **safe space** for her, in which she could let go and relax her body, remembering to breathe and to trust the internal cues and impulses that were energy and information in flow: not stopping that flow of energy, as the body re-wired itself.

For a brief period, I was able be my mother's 'Guardian', enabling her to remember her own genius at the age of 88. Rather than a person bogged down and twisted with worry and limiting beliefs of being incapacitated and 'stuck' with her lot in life; feelings of having to put up and shut up and make the best of things; feelings of being small and puny and old and somehow therefore without worth. These were thoughts that prevented her from continuing to access her own potential. Once she remembered the grand, powerful lady that she was, and was becoming again, she didn't have to put up with anyone being rude or abusive or downright disrespectful to her, ever again. She was standing up for herself: she had reclaimed her dignity of choice, the birthright of her own potential. A boundless potential that never diminishes, no matter what the age! It is never too late!

Noreen Mejias - MBA, CFP, CIM, FCSI, EPC, Ch.P., CODE Model Coach™ - has been in the financial services industry since 1986. As a Chartered Professional *Strategic Wealth* Advisor (Ch.P.) she uses a consultative holistic approach to forge deep meaningful relationships with her clients. She builds trust by demonstrating genuine, bias-free and diverse wealth management expertise in creating strategic solutions for the often-complex needs of individuals, families and business owners through all life stages.

With impressive credentials, well-honed skills and the wisdom that comes with experience, she is both willing and able to work with you as coach, guide and catalyst to strengthen, protect and enhance your resources and quality of life, as a gateway to expansive majestic living.

THE COURAGE TO CHOOSE DIFFERENTLY
Louise LeBrun

Reading the chapters of this book offers us a glimpse into the lives of those who see through very different eyes, inviting us to consider how else we might see ourselves, our world and our way of moving through it. These stories are invitations rather than command performances, leaving it to each of us to determine where we go from here.

I am reminded that no matter what the circumstances, there is always hope for us all - for our ourselves, for our children and for our individual and collective futures - because, in truth, we are the co-creators of it all! In these pages, it has become clear that any hope must be seeded in the unfolding of *our own* evolution - first! - and not left waiting for the evolution of something 'out there', be it person, place or event. We *are* the fecund space within which life's potential sits in anticipation of its taking root, breaking through the coma of our self-imposed limitations and bursting through the soil of our uncertainty into the warmth of the sun. It is up to each of us to determine how we grow and how we influence the growth of others.

You can choose to allow those tentative and fragile 'knowings' inside you to move you to engage differently; or you can choose to do nothing and continue your life as it is currently unfolding. Either way, your life will become the evidence... the popcorn trail... that reveals to you and the world the choices you have made. (In a world that is obsessed with 'privacy' and 'secrecy', we are far more obvious than we think!) It takes great courage to be willing to not know and move forward, anyway.

We have the ability to shape our children in ways that allow them to stand tall and reach for the sky; or in ways that stunt their growth and cripple them in body, mind and spirit. As in all things in life, it is a choice - and as powerful forces in the lives of our children, it starts with the choices we make for ourselves.

Far beyond yet another set of practices and techniques to impose on our children, the voices of this book speak of and to us as the forces that shape culture. They carry wise words representing lessons learned, new roads taken and lives changed; and offer invitations to reconsider our own lives so that we can discover something more powerful, waiting patiently within ourselves.

Whether parents of very young children (like Anita and Naomi) or young adults (like Ray, Amy and Marie); whether grandmothers actively engaged in the shaping of new worlds (like Cathy, Pat and Lucy); or whether Wise Women choosing to share the insights of their own awakening journey for the benefit of others - both as adult and child (like Debbie and Noreen), what they all have in common is the realization that it all begins with them... deep inside... where they live. Without that singular and potent awareness, lives are ruined in our misguided belief that someone else (someone wiser, smarter, older; someone in charge or 'in the know'; our experts, specialists and professionals) will 'fix' it or take care of it. In our endless waiting, we slowly fade away.

Taking responsibility for our highly personal impact on the lives of others is not an easy thing to do. We have been conditioned (intergenerationally) to look outside ourselves for reasons and solutions only to ultimately discover that we are at the root of the quality of our own lives! To look inside and own what's there takes great courage and a willingness to trust the magnificence of our imperfection.

As you move forward from this day, remember to:

- **Trust your body** ~ Your body never lies. Unlike what many of us have been taught to believe, not only is your body not the enemy, it is in fact the gateway to the transformation that we seek. All we need to do is surrender the intellect to the body and let the body lead. Our greatest challenge is getting out of our own way!

- **Breathe** ~ Begin by paying attention to your breathing and notice when you hold your breath. In that moment, just stop… close your eyes... and take three or four long, slow, deep breaths. If you extend the exhale so that it is twice as long as the inhale, you'll go a long way to creating a deep state of relaxation in the body. In that state, you cannot feel fear – and when we are unafraid, we are more willing and able to consider new information and new experiences.

- **Follow the Impulse** ~ The next time your body 'feels' something, instead of trying to shut down or move away from that sensation/impulse, breathe; relax your body; and choose to move into the sensation rather than away from it. What you've been taught to call 'emotions' are really waves of energy/information trying to be metabolized (like your lunch) in the quantum biological processor that your body is, so that you can get on with your life! With the integration of each wave of information come insights and discoveries. Life changes – quickly, easily, effortlessly - and there is no going back.

- **Tell the truth** ~ Even if you never say it out loud to another soul, tell yourself the truth – inside you, where you live. We lie to ourselves all the time. We tell ourselves that something doesn't matter, when it does; that we're willing to do something when we're not; or that we want something when we don't. When we allow ourselves to claim the truth of our own experience, something powerful happens inside of us and in that moment, we can access more of our own potential.

- **Stay in the tough conversations** ~ The toughest conversation you'll ever have to stay in is the one with yourself. When you consider that there are only two things going on in the world - the conversations you have with yourself, and the conversations you have with another human being (i.e. chats, email, reports, etc); and when you consider that you can't change the one you have with another person unless and until you're both willing and able to change the one you have with yourself, staying in that tough conversation with YOU will determine the quality of your life!

- **Be willing to stand alone** ~ Far too often in life we go along just to get along. We compromise ourselves because we think that if we really let others see who we are, they'll move away from us. And yet, when we do that, we end up not liking ourselves much and have already moved away from ourselves. When we become both willing (a choice) and able (see the previous four points) to stand alone, we discover as we look around that there are many others who seek the same quality of life. These folks indeed, make great playmates.

As you engage your life in this way, you'll begin to discover that you are much more than you ever dreamed possible – and it all comes from discovering that your body is not the enemy. You can relax into and trust your body to gently guide you home.

Moving Forward

Where do you go from here? How do you now put one foot in front of the other in a useful and purposeful way, knowing that the journey is your own to design? How do you discover how to engage differently and trust that you are not alone in doing so?

The Courage to Choose Differently

What each of the contributing authors shares is the ability to live in a new paradigm... a new context for experiencing themselves and others in a more life-altering and meaningful way. Each has taken the journey that has awakened discovery of the innate genius that sits just below the surface of habit and cultural conditioning. In the authentic living of their own lives, contribution to others becomes possible. You can't give what you haven't got!; and in that, each has dared to dream that they could indeed, be more authentically themselves.

It doesn't have to be hard and it doesn't have to cost a lot of money. There are many things that you can begin to do - right now! - that will require only the investment of your time and attention. Visit the WEL-Systems® Institute website to find what you are looking for.

- Begin by reading *Fully Alive: Awakening Health, Humor, Compassion and Truth*; and listening to the 2-CD program *Pathways to Personal Power*. These seminal works in the WEL-Systems body of knowledge will offer information, insight and a framework for discovery that will become your gateway to awakening to how else you might live.

- Take the time to connect with the authors who have touched something in you. They are very welcoming of contact with you and are both willing and able to engage with you to accelerate your own evolution.

- Many of the authors have online blogs to which they are regular contributors. You can access their blogs from the Institute site.

- You'll discover an abundance of free articles on a wide range of subjects from health and wellness to leadership, money and spirituality. You'll find these listed under Free Articles.

- Subscribe to the RSS feeds for ChoicePoints, the free online newsletter. Stay connected to new thoughts, new experiences, new products and new insights through articles, products and events.

- Choose from the available CD experiences that range from single CD/single topic programs to multi-CD collections offering more in-depth exploration on life's interests and challenges. Take the plunge and discover more of yourself in the privacy of your own mind. All of the WEL-Systems CDs are available to purchase online.

- When you're ready to dive into the deep end of the pool, consider being part of a small-group, guided process of discovery. WEL-Systems based experiences are available from introductory evenings to multi-day intensives and retreats, masterfully facilitated by the people - just like you! - who have chosen to take back their lives in a more meaningful way. You'll find a Schedule and list of possible programs on the Institute website.

- Many of the contributing authors offer a range of programs/services/experiences that will help you, help yourself. Take the time to visit the Information Pages for *Guardians of the Vision* and explore who, what, where, when and how you can connect with these Certified CODE Model Coaches™ for individual and/or small-group experiences (in person, online or by phone) to begin your journey of discovery.

These are challenging times - and in this challenge, we must find ourselves and each other. Far too many of us are lost to ourselves and our potential; and far too many are left to stand alone and in isolation to fend for our children when we can barely fend for ourselves.

Guardianship of the vision... of the birthright that is an expression of the soul... knows no boundaries of age, creed, color or economics. It is not bound by history or social status; by the merciless judgements of ourselves and each other; or by the limitations of our past, the despair of our present or the fear of our future. Like we are discovering that Gaia needs all of us to awaken, so our children - the ones we have been and the ones who live on through us and with us - need all of us to embrace the journey of discovery of our own potential that we might have the willingness and ability to help them discover their own.

It starts with you: with this breath, this moment, this thought and this choice. It moves forward, one moment to the next, being wiling to invite and allow... and trust that if you're drawn to seek more, there is a reason for that. It accelerates when you become willing to trust the truth of your own experience... to trust your body and allow it to lead! And it changes the world when you and I become willing and able to be ourselves... that authentic presence that lives deep inside, longing to free itself from history, habit and cultural imposition... that we might design a different world.

Telling yourself the truth is an act of courage. Telling your truth out loud, in the presence of others, is an act of transformation!

Louise LeBrun is the Founder of the WEL-Systems Institute and creator of the ever-growing and profoundly effective WEL-Systems® body of knowledge including Quantum TLC™, The CODE Model™ and CODE Model Coaching™.

A visionary and an activist, Louise is a cutting-edge thinker, writer, speaker, educator and Awakened Living Coach. Her unwavering commitment to her own evolution has been the key to maintaining a cutting-edge perspective on human evolution. Her willingness to transform her personal discoveries into simple and accessible processes for others, makes it possible for you to accelerate your own evolution with less effort and outstanding results.

REFLECTIONS

If I had known then what I know now

I would have known that any prescribed role I played whether it was "Working Mom" or "Stay at Home Mom" was far too small to define who I am. I would have freed myself to live a great, big, juicy life that reflects who I really am - sooner.

Anita Allen

...especially the incredible power I carried to impact my chidrens' future, I would have parented more resourcefully. Now, no longer a parent, yet still a mother, I carry the ability to influence those to whom I gave birth, and others by my willingness to choose consciously and resourcefully for my own future

Cathy Carmody

I would have lived my life as I am now! An authentic life in the moment, every moment, completely decloaked and without fear! Consciously choosing and choosing again, standing in the moment and imagining how much bigger and more meaningful my life can be by living an Emerging Future.

Patricia Donihee

I would not have spent years trying to fit into a box that others built. I would have had the courage to stand alone being who I am, instead of twisting, bending and contorting to be everything that others thought I should be.

Debbie Elliott

I would have relaxed and trusted myself to be just fine, no matter what! I would have laughed more, cried more. I would have felt my way through things from the inside out instead of thinking my way through my life. I would have asked all the questions that went unexplored. I would have showed up and spoken up and allowed the roar in my belly to make its way to my mouth and into my world. I would have relished being me!

Lucy Hensel

I would not have lost myself in the 'role' of mother. I would have honored myself knowing in doing so I was teaching my children to honor themselves. I would have laughed more, cried more, sung more and allowed myself to Be more in the presence of my children.

Naomi Irons-Hill

I would have sought more healing for myself, more experiences for personal growth and information about who I was beyond the conventional notions of man, and who it was possible for me to become as a person, before I took on the role of parenting.

Ray Landry

I would have lived - unedited! - trusting that I was safe. I would have embraced my feral nature... that which is held as so dangerous and threatening to 'civilized' society... recognizing that creativity and innovation more often than not require that we take a big bite out of the status quo!

Louise LeBrun

I would have unhesitatingly stepped over my limiting beliefs that much sooner and acknowledged to mySelf that what I create and have to share is truly meaningful and does make a difference. I would have welcomed and honoured the fact that my contribution to Life is what lights me up and gives me my raison d'etre!

Noreen Mejias

I would have not been willing to ever question my own intelligence (gut instinct) because of someone else's' opinion. Now as I stand tall in who I am, my daughter gets to do the same.

Amy McNaughton

I know I am no longer the 'lone wolf'. Those days of dancing around 'silencing' and 'isolating' myself are over. Moment to moment, this gift I have given myself, is rippling out into my world, allowing my son, as well as my clients, to reclaim who they are and becoming in the world! How amazing is that!

Marie Smith

 *Evolution by Intention*™

In order to progress beyond historical notions of evolution through incremental change, to one of *Evolution by Intention* we must first:

- redefine who we are as human beings and how we experience our humanity
- rediscover and reclaim what has always been there, reawakening to our existing genius and potential to shape our world

Who we must continue to become:

- Leaders of global transformation
- An opportunity to engage life differently through:
  - a call to women to lead and co-create with men differently
  - an invitation for men to relax into new ways of being
- A 'wave' or 'movement' for creating living, organic collectives that thrive on the uniqueness of the individual and his/her impact when choosing to 'Engage!'
- A living model for manifestation of a future based on standing in the moment, looking into the future and creating by intention

How we must choose:

We make the choices that will move us toward our declared intention and to not make choices that will simply move us away from our fears.

Our declared beliefs/values/attitudes:

★ History (the past) is irrelevant as a guide to creating the future
★ I live in a holographic universe
★ I am a Quantum Biological Human
★ Growth is a biological imperative
★ I am critical to making a difference
★ It's not too late
★ I am up to the challenge
★ There is an urgency to engage
★ If not me, then who?
★ This is fun, exciting and adventurous: I don't have to do serious things, seriously
★ I am the godforce expressing in a physical universe
★ My world is a safe and abundant place
★ My confusion is a gateway/portal to my own evolution
★ I am not alone
★ My 'reality' is malleable based on my expectations
★ What you think of me is none of my business
★ Every response is an intelligent response: there are no exceptions!
★ Your judgments of me are reflections of your internal landscapes
★ When I engage, a difference occurs
★ My power is in the size and courage of my questions

Are you ready to transform your life?

Are you passionate about working with others as they seek to accelerate their evolution?

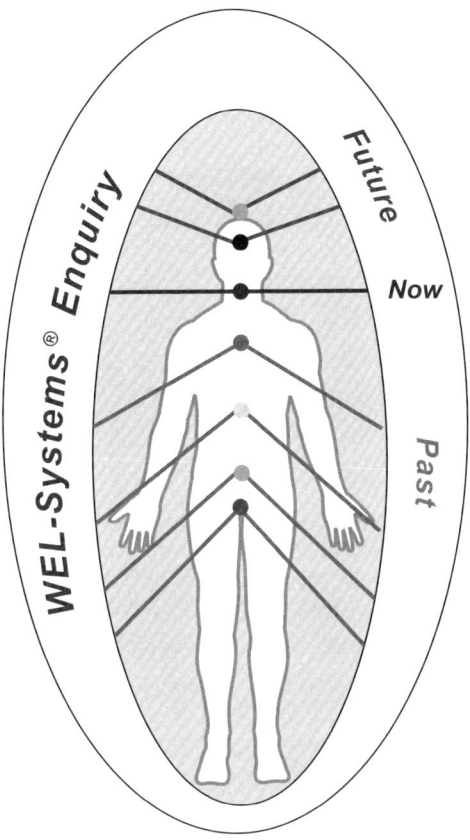

CODE Model Coaching™ is not a practice or a technique - it's a way of being. It's an experience that is grounded in a new paradigm that becomes the invitation for self and other to continue to grow and evolve, accessing human potential in ways that translate to practical living and a heightened quality of human experience. For more information, visit the WEL-Systems Institute web site.

Join other women who are changing their world!

The WEL-Systems® Institute

The WEL-Systems Institute is a world leader in life-altering and generative change programs, products and experiences for accelerated consciousness and personal evolution all created in a WEL-Systems® context. The Institute is at the core of an evolving global collective, built on the strength of the individuality of its members and a desire to further evolve in the company of others on a similar journey of discovery.

For more information and to explore what else is available, please visit the web site at **www.WEL-Systems.com**. The site is up-dated regularly to provide you with information on new experiences, articles, books, audio products, and a schedule of events.

Contact us by email at: info@WEL-Systems.com
or call us at: 1-613-254-7218